Keto Made Easy

100+ EASY KETO DISHES MADE FAST to Fit Your Life

MEGHA BAROT and MATT GAEDKE

VICTOR BELT PUBLISHING

Las Vegas

From Matt:

To my parents, Margaret and Richard, and my friends, Tarik, Adam, and Lou—
You're the average of the five people you spend the most time with.

From Megha:

To my dad, Ashok, and my best friend, Kelsey—
You have helped me realize that we never have life figured out,
and that's okay. Eat good food, and be happy.

First Published in 2018 by Victory Belt Publishing Inc.

Copyright © 2018 by Megha Barot and Matt Gaedke

ISBN-13: 978-1-628602-88-3

Front and Back Cover Photography by Kala Snow

Cover Design by Justin-Aaron Velasco

Interior Design by Yordan Terziev and Boryana Yordanova

Printed in Canada

TC 0318

CONTENTS

PREFACE

If you are holding this book and reading this preface, we want to say thank you. We hope you are excited to enter into this world of recipes that we have created for you in which you can indulge, guilt-free! We are Matt and Megha, and we make up KetoConnect. We run a food blog specific to a low-carb, ketogenic diet. We also have a YouTube channel that gives a glimpse into our lives with our pets, Miley and Julius, but, more importantly, shows you exactly how to make our recipes step by step, how to be prepared and successful in your keto lifestyle, and how to adapt as your body does.

Before we even met, we always had a passion for food, both for cooking it and for eating it. In particular, we loved Asian takeout and desserts, but we also highly valued our health. So we met at the crossroads of enjoying sweets and other comfort foods regularly and staying strict and doing what we knew—or, should we say, *thought*—was "good for us." But why not have both?

Shortly after meeting one another in San Francisco, we discovered the ketogenic diet and decided to give it a go together. We quit carbs cold turkey and got hit with the keto flu—bad! But a short time later, we noticed the exact opposite, with heightened energy and focus being two of the main benefits of our newfound lifestyle. (And since then, we've learned that the keto flu can be avoided or lessened through supplementation with the three major electrolytes—sodium, magnesium, and potassium—or by tapering down carb consumption as opposed to going cold turkey like we did.)

Once we started to cook with new ingredients and think a little differently about the food we put into our bodies, everything else in our lives changed as well. We ate out less and were more careful about what we consumed, but we still indulged in delicious homemade meals and desserts. Our love for eating higher-quality food and living a healthier lifestyle turned into more than just our bonding time; it became our business, too. We thought, "Hey, what's stopping us from cooking, taking pictures, and posting it all on the internet for others to benefit?"

Well, at the time, a lot. We had no means of making this happen. However, when Matt took the initial step of buying our first camera and the second step of buying the domain name KetoConnect.net, things started to become a little clearer.

Although nothing happened overnight, we continued to research the diet, fight about recipes (Megha preferred simple recipes, while Matt liked to overdo it with spices and other ingredients), burn all the desserts we made, and put in countless hours after coming home from our full-time jobs. Sure enough, we started to make a little progress. Everything wonderful in life takes time, and we are big advocates of enjoying the entire journey. If we hadn't put our heads down, focused, and kept working toward our goal of building KetoConnect, you wouldn't be holding this cookbook today.

With this book, we want to let you in on the idea that you can have it both ways: you can value your health and indulge in delicious foods, too. That is why we made sure to include all the foods we miss from our high-carb days, as well as the recipes that help us stay on track and on budget. The recipes in this book are designed to make the entire process a little easier, which is why we named the book *Keto Made Easy*.

Our goal is to provide you with a foundation of recipes from all categories, ranging from takeout favorites to desserts. We have found cooking to be an intimate and relaxing experience, and we want to give you those same feelings. No matter how busy our days are—and sometimes we are working nonstop—we like to take at least ten minutes to make a meal worth eating or drinking! We know many of you are busy, too, or always on the go, so we have made it a point to include several quick-to-make recipes and recipes that you can meal prep for the week. However, we also know that many of you have families and have found cooking to be an enjoyable part of your keto journey, so we also give you the option to make more involved recipes, sure to satisfy even the pickiest kids! Most of our recipes are a great starting point for adding your own twists, and we always encourage a little experimentation. That's where the magic happens!

A lot of our motivation has come from our viewers and supporters. We've grown not only as individuals and as a business, but also in our ability to learn from you and then apply that knowledge as we develop new recipes that you can easily re-create and enjoy. We want cooking to be fun, lighthearted, and approachable. We want to inspire the chef within you to make our Southern Baked Chicken (page 118) and our Death by Chocolate Cheesecake (page 210), because you can live your healthiest life and indulge a little, too!

HOW TO USE THE RECIPES IN THIS BOOK

More and more people are cutting out carbs in hopes of losing weight, increasing energy, and performing better mentally and physically. Just about everyone has tried it at some point, but it can be hard to stick to for the long haul. There's always a holiday or some other special occasion around the corner, and you know what that means: Mom's fried chicken, your aunt's homemade dinner rolls, or Grandma's rhubarb crisp. For every occasion there is a special food that you just can't pass up; it's tradition.

That's where this book comes in. It's loaded with keto-friendly versions of your favorite foods and should be used to supplement your keto diet in a way that makes it more sustainable. Rather than stopping to pick up a pint of ice cream on your way home from work, make one of the delicious desserts in this book. This book is jammed full of better choices!

Quick Reference Icons

We've included quick reference icons in our recipes to designate whether they meet certain dietary restrictions. We have icons for recipes that are dairy-free, egg-free, nut-free, and/or vegetarian. For the sake of labeling, we consider coconut products, such as coconut flour, coconut milk, and coconut flakes, to be nut-free. We have found that those who have allergies to nuts generally do not have issues with coconut.

DAIRY-FREE

EGG-FREE

NUT-FREE

VEGETARIAN

There are a number of foolproof recipes included in this book. These are the easiest recipes in the book and require very little experience in the kitchen. Look for this icon:

 **FOOLPROOF**

If you're unfamiliar with the concept, meal prep is the practice of making meals in bulk, often on the weekend, so that you'll have ready-to-eat meals throughout the week. This happens to be our number-one tip for success on a keto diet. Be on the lookout for this icon; you will find it accompanying those recipes that are particularly well suited to meal prep.

 **MEAL PREP**

Ingredients

In the "Ingredients and Kitchen Tips" section that begins on page 12, we walk you through the ingredients we use in our daily cooking. We've accumulated quite an assortment of exotic ingredients since we started our blog, but we like to keep it simple in most of our recipes. You should be able to find everything you need to make the recipes in this book at your local grocery store, except for a couple of items that can easily be found online.

Twists

We'll be the first ones to tell you that our recipes are awesome. Each of them has been carefully tested until it's perfect. But that doesn't mean you shouldn't add your own signature occasionally! Recipes are best used as a framework within which to experiment, adding your own touches and changing ingredients to suit your tastes. In that spirit, we've included some of our favorite twists on classic recipes throughout the book. You'll find them at the ends of the recipes, along with other important notes and helpful tips.

Nutritional Information

For each recipe, we've listed the total calories along with the number of grams of fat, protein, carbohydrate, fiber, and sugar alcohol, where applicable. Erythritol is a non-nutritive sweetener that is commonly used in low-carb cooking. Because it does not impact blood glucose levels in most people, it is subtracted from the total carb count of the recipe.

It's important to note that these nutritional values were calculated based on the brands of ingredients we used; there may be slight variations if you opt for different products. We did our best to ensure the accuracy of our calculations, but if you are using a ketogenic diet to treat a medical condition, it is important that you calculate the nutritional values of each recipe for yourself. Also, please keep in mind that optional ingredients are not included in the nutritional information.

INGREDIENTS AND KITCHEN TIPS

In this section, we highlight the ingredients that are staples in our cooking, as well as some of the brands we prefer. For a complete list of our brand recommendations for staple ingredients, turn to the "Resource Guide" section on pages 280 to 282.

Please note that when shopping for dairy products, you should always buy the full-fat versions. Also, check to make sure that any prepared or canned foods you purchase do not contain added sugars. Always read the labels when buying ingredients, especially those that are unfamiliar to you.

Flours and Fibers

This section explores the flours and fibers that we use in our day-to-day cooking and baking. If you're unfamiliar with low-carb baking, this list will serve as a starter course on the commonly used ingredients.

We use two types of flour:

- **Almond flour** is one of the most commonly used grain-free and gluten-free flour substitutes. We always buy finely ground blanched almond flour as opposed to coarsely ground almond flour or almond meal. A finer grind yields the best, most consistent results. Our go-to brand is Bob's Red Mill.

- **Coconut flour** is another great option for low-carb baking. Our go-to brand is Anthony's Goods. It is important to note that coconut flour is dramatically different from almond flour. Coconut flour is much more absorbent, and for this reason it is very hard to use one of these flours in place of the other. A good general rule when substituting one for the other is to use three-and-a-half parts almond flour for every one part of coconut flour, but even then, there is no guarantee that the recipe will turn out well.

We use three different types of fiber for baking. Because each type has a different absorbency and texture, it is best to use the specific type of fiber the recipe calls for. Substituting one type for another is possible, but the results will not be nearly as good.

- **Psyllium husk powder** is a high-fiber powder that can be used in tandem with coconut flour to achieve a fluffy consistency in keto baked goods. Depending on the brand you use, it can turn breads gray or purple. We use the NOW Foods brand, which we've found has a great taste and does not discolor our baked goods.

- **Oat fiber** lends itself more to cakes, cookies, and other desserts than to breads. It has a faint oatmeal flavor and can be delicious when used properly. Our go-to brand is Anthony's Goods.

- **Flax meal** is made from ground flax seeds. It is less absorbent than the other two fibers and creates a more wheatlike baked good with a toasted flavor. We use both golden and regular flax meal in our recipes; the two are interchangeable. The only difference is flavor. That said, we often prefer the more assertive and "toasty" flavor of golden flax meal and specify it in those recipes in which we think it is best suited. However, feel free to substitute one type for the other, depending on what you have on hand. Our go-to brand for both types of flax meal is Bob's Red Mill.

Sweeteners

There are several keto-friendly sweeteners available. The main ones we like to use are erythritol and liquid stevia, both of which have a very low glycemic index and have not been shown to have a negative impact on ketosis.

- **Erythritol** is a sugar alcohol that looks just like table sugar and is 70 percent as sweet. A number of different sugar alcohols are used in low-carb baking, but erythritol is our favorite due to its low glycemic index and pleasant taste. If you've never used it before, know that it can have a slight cooling effect in your mouth. Erythritol comes in a granular form but can easily be ground to a powder in a coffee or spice grinder. We use both granular and powdered erythritol in our recipes. Certain recipes call for powdered erythritol because the granular form won't yield the same result. For example, the granular form would make sauces and frostings gritty. Our go-to brand of erythritol is Anthony's Goods.

- **Liquid stevia** is a natural sweetener extracted from the leaves of the stevia plant. It is our favorite sweetener, and we use it daily in our morning coffee. A couple drops do the trick! We prefer the liquid form over the granular form because granular stevia typically contains bulking agents that are high in carbohydrates. If you are unaccustomed to using stevia, you will likely find that it has a slightly bitter aftertaste. This can be lessened by using a smaller amount and combining it with some erythritol to achieve your preferred sweetness level. From our experience, 1 teaspoon of erythritol is equivalent to about 5 drops of liquid stevia. Our go-to liquid stevia product is NOW Foods Better Stevia.

- **Swerve Confectioners** is a convenient option for any recipe that calls for powdered erythritol. It saves you the step of powdering erythritol yourself, but it is more expensive than granular erythritol. To save money, we grind granular erythritol to a powder ourselves.

- **Sugar-free maple syrup** is not our favorite ingredient to use because it tends to contain unsavory artificial sweeteners, but it does provide a great maple flavor, along with a thick consistency that lends itself very well to certain recipes. Unfortunately, it is hard to replicate sugar-free maple syrup; however, Know Foods makes a great sugar-free maple-flavored syrup that is free of those unsavory sweeteners.

We find it advantageous to have one form of powdered sweetener and one form of liquid sweetener to use for sweetening foods and drinks. When making smoothies and our morning coffee, we prefer liquid stevia, and for baking, we prefer powdered erythritol.

Fresh and Dried Herbs and Spices

Using fresh herbs sometimes adds a depth of flavor that you might not be able to achieve by using dried herbs. Soups are a good example. However, when a recipe calls for fresh herbs, feel free to substitute dried herbs if those are all you have on hand. The ratio for subbing dried herbs for fresh ones is one part dried herbs to three parts fresh.

Here is a list of the herbs and spices that we use most often in this book.

Dried herbs:

- Oregano leaves
- Parsley
- Rosemary leaves

Fresh herbs:

- Basil
- Chives
- Cilantro
- Sage

Spices:

- Cayenne pepper
- Chili powder
- Curry powder
- Garlic powder
- Ginger powder
- Ground cinnamon
- Ground cumin
- Onion powder
- Paprika
- Red pepper flakes

Salt

For cooking and baking, our preferred type of salt is finely ground pink Himalayan salt.

Nut and Peanut Butters

When purchasing nut and peanut butters, we try to go the natural route. Natural usually means that no sugars are added. Many popular brands contain added sugars, upping the carb count per serving, and many almond butters contain palm oil. Your best bet when buying peanut or nut butter is to read the ingredient list to ensure that there are no additives. The only ingredients you want to see listed are the nut (or peanuts, which are legumes) or, at most, nuts and salt. Our preferred brand of peanut butter is Crazy Richard's. We don't have a favorite brand of almond butter; we simply check the ingredient list to make sure that it's 100 percent almonds (again, salt is okay).

In all the recipes in this book that call for peanut or nut butter, we used unsalted; if you use a salted peanut or nut butter, we recommend that you reduce the amount of salt called for in the recipe.

Protein Powders

When a recipe calls for protein powder, whatever you have on hand will likely work just fine. However, some recipes work best when you use a whey-based protein powder; for those recipes, we specify whey protein powder. When purchasing protein powder, we like to find the lowest-carb option, with at most 3 grams of carbohydrate per scoop.

- **Flavored protein powders** are a convenient way to add flavor and sweetness to recipes. Our favorite all-purpose product is Isopure zero/low-carb protein powder. It is whey-based and comes in eleven different flavors (our favorite is Cookies & Cream). For our Instant Protein Ice Cream (page 240), however, we like to use Quest brand flavored protein powders; the mix of whey and casein protein in Quest's powders gives our ice cream a creamier texture. Aside from that, the flavor of your protein powder is a personal preference. Just remember that the flavor of the protein powder you use generally dictates the flavor of the food you are making.

- **Unflavored protein powders** are a great way to up the protein as well as provide bulk when baking. However, unflavored protein powder does not have any sweetener in it. When using the unflavored type, it is advisable to add sweetener, such as liquid stevia. Our favorite unflavored protein powder is Isopure's whey protein isolate.

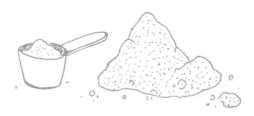

Chocolate

We use two main types of chocolate in our recipes: unsweetened baking chocolate and sugar-free chocolate chips. While both types can be found in many grocery stores, baking chocolate is more widely available.

- **Unsweetened baking chocolate** is 100 percent cacao; therefore, it has no sweetness. Although it works great as a substitute for sugar-free chocolate chips when chopped into chunks, it generally requires the addition of more sweetener. We like to add some liquid stevia when working with baking chocolate to ensure that the finished dish has the right level of sweetness. We use this product more often because it is more widely available and less expensive than other chocolate options.

- **Sugar-free chocolate chips** are great for cookies, loaves, and anything baked with chocolate. Be aware, though, that not all sugar-free chocolate chips are sweetened with quality keto-friendly sweeteners. Avoid chocolate chips sweetened with cane sugar, coconut sugar, or maltitol, as well as any product that uses the bulking agent maltodextrin. Our favorite brand of sugar-free chocolate chips is Lily's, which are sweetened with erythritol and stevia and contain no added sugar. The downside is that they are pricey.

Nondairy Milk

When a recipe calls for a nondairy milk, such as almond milk, you can substitute any type of nondairy milk you have on hand. Some examples we've used in our baking and cooking are cashew milk, coconut milk, and flax milk. We've found that flax milk most closely resembles cow's milk in flavor. When purchasing nondairy milk, always buy the unsweetened variety, which is the lowest in carbs. You can always add your own sweetener and extract at home when using the milk in baking recipes.

Oils and Fats

The oil we use most often is refined coconut oil. It can be replaced with ghee in any recipe. Both refined coconut oil and ghee have a high smoke point, which is why they are our preferred fats for cooking and frying. We also like to use coconut oil spray for greasing a baking dish or skillet without adding calories. Coconut oil spray can be found in the baking section of any grocery store.

Here are some other tips about keto-friendly oils and fats:

- **Avocado oil** is a great substitute for olive oil, particularly when you want a more neutral flavor.

- **Coconut oil** is a great substitute for butter.

- **Lard** is a handy option for frying.

Kitchen Tips

Here are some various tips to keep in mind as you prepare the recipes in this book.

Bring ingredients to room temperature where noted.

When a recipe calls for room-temperature ingredients, it is important to allow them to warm to room temperature prior to using them. This ensures that everything will come together uniformly.

Know that different brands of an ingredient can affect the outcome of a recipe.

On pages 280 to 282, we've provided you with our go-to brands for the products that we've found tend to vary from brand to brand. These brands are the ones we use most often in our kitchen and have been the most thoroughly tested. If you use another brand, the consistency and texture of the finished dish may vary slightly.

Preheat the oven.

Always preheat your oven and allow it to reach temperature before putting food in it; otherwise, you might see different results.

Flatten cookies before baking where indicated.

Some cookies, especially those made with coconut flour, won't spread in the oven. When a recipe instructs you to do so, it is important to flatten the cookies using your hands or a fork prior to baking. If you don't flatten them, they may not cook through fully.

Remember that oven temperatures vary.

Temperatures vary from one oven to another, so it's important to take note of the cook time ranges indicated in the recipes as well as the descriptions of doneness provided. To prevent foods from burning, keep an eye on anything you put in the oven and begin checking for doneness at the start of the cook time range.

Make your own coconut cream.

You can buy cans of unsweetened coconut cream (we prefer the Thai Kitchen brand), or you can extract coconut cream from a can of full-fat coconut milk. To do that, place the can of coconut milk in the fridge for a full 24 hours. After 24 hours, open the can and, using a spoon, scoop out the cream, which will be about the top 90 percent of the contents of the can. The coconut water will have separated from the cream and will be left at the bottom of the can. If you accidentally get a little of the water while scooping out the cream, don't worry; it is unlikely that a minimal amount will affect the recipe.

Store foods safely.

We store opened flours and fibers in tightly sealed zip-top plastic bags, with all the air removed, to keep them as fresh as possible in our pantry. We store fresh herbs in the refrigerator for up to a week. Oils and fats can be stored in the fridge as well, if desired, but will do just fine stored on a shelf in a cool, dry place.

FIVE STEPS TO STARTING KETO

1. Cut the carbs.

Cutting carbs could mean gradually reducing them over weeks or months or cutting them all at once. An important step is to become aware of how many carbs are in different foods and to become skilled at tracking your carb intake. A good starting place for keto is 20 grams of net carbs per day. Net carbs are simply total carbs minus fiber (both of which are listed on food packaging in the United States). Keeping that number under 20 grams per day will put your body into a state of ketosis. Reducing your carb intake is essential to your success on keto and should definitely be the first line item that you address.

TIP:

Develop a rotation of five to seven staple meals. Doing so allows you to easily know the nutrition of those meals; plus, you get really good at making those dishes after a while.

2. Brace yourself.

The first week on keto is tough. Your body is doing something completely new and is trying to rewire circuitry that has been in place for your entire life. Learning to run on fat is worth it, but the transition is a rough one. Most people feel extremely fatigued and low on energy for the first three to five days. These symptoms can be mitigated with supplementation, but even then you're going to feel a bit different. We promise that this feeling will pass! Around the five- to seven-day mark, "keto clarity" will hit and you will feel like a new person.

TIP:

Supplementing with electrolytes is important on a keto diet and can help mitigate some of the adaptation symptoms. Make sure to get sodium in the form of salt; potassium from avocados, broccoli, spinach, and supplements; and magnesium from nuts, spinach, dark chocolate, and supplements. Drinking lots of water also will help.

3. Add some fat.

Eating high-fat is counterintuitive for all of us who were raised during the low-fat boom. Our underlying fear of fat will need to be conquered in our quest for health. When starting a keto diet, most people are good about cutting carbs, but they fail to add fat. This results in a high-protein diet, which is going to leave you with low energy and wanting to run back to your carbs. Actively seeking out fat will result in much better energy levels, better hunger control, and an overall more sustainable diet. Fat is your new energy source. Don't be afraid of energy!

TIP:

Butter coffee and tea are a huge help for adding fat to your diet. So are fat bombs. Fat bombs can be eaten in place of dessert or as a side at meals to increase the fat content.

4. Time your meals.

Once you've got the first three steps down, it's time to do some fine-tuning. Ditching the standard breakfast, snack, lunch, snack, dinner, dessert paradigm can be liberating! Don't confine yourself to the typical eating windows. Experiment with different schedules that match up with your lifestyle. Skip breakfast one day. ("But it's the most important meal of the day!" said the cereal company.) Eat just one meal a day. Try eating nothing but fat until 2 or 3 p.m. (that's what Megha does). Don't be afraid to stray from societal norms around meal timing. After all, early humans didn't enter starvation mode if they didn't get their potato chips every two hours!

TIP:

Most people are not hungry when they first wake up. Listen to your body and eat in accordance with what it's telling you.

5. Continually improve.

Three years into our keto diet, we continue to improve and change things up almost weekly. We view it as a challenge: add something new, see how our bodies react, adjust the next week. View this as a never-ending process, especially if you're coming straight from the standard American diet. If the Big Mac wrapper from last night is still on the passenger seat of your car, it's probably not feasible for you to switch to a completely whole-foods diet today. Baby steps. Maybe switch out the Big Mac for a Big Mac with no bun. That's easy, right? Get yourself some low-carb ice cream from the grocery store. Do the best you can. Tomorrow you will be able to do a little bit better. Think of where you'll be in a year!

TIP:

Perfection is often the enemy of improvement. If you think you need to be perfect with your diet from day one, chances are you'll never even start. The way we started a keto diet was by subbing out high-carb options for low-carb replacements and continually improving from there.

KEYS TO SUCCESS

PREP YOUR MEALS AHEAD

One of Matt's favorite sayings is "if you fail to prepare, you prepare to fail," and preparation is something we strongly believe in, especially when you're new to a keto lifestyle! It can be hard to know what to eat and in what proportions. We've found that the best way to beat this is bulk meal prepping. Planning and preparing your meals over the weekend for the week ahead gives you the flexibility to create the menu of your choosing, being sure to hit your ideal macros each day. It also makes eating a lot less stressful: all your meals are already made, so all you have to do is heat and eat!

We understand, however, that you or members of your family may not like to eat the same thing every day. In that case, another good option is to prep just one item, like a meat. If you prepped our Crispy Chicken Thighs with Pan Sauce (page 108) on Sunday, for example, you could chop up the meat to add to meals throughout the week, such as salads, a stir-fry, or our Curry Chicken Salad (page 160). You could even prep our Raspberry Fiber Muffins (page 78) to take to work for breakfast or a snack each day!

Another great option for staying on track is to have something sweet on hand at all times to satisfy your cravings, or if you know you're going to want a sweet treat while you watch the season premiere of *The Bachelor.* We like to make our Chocolate Peanut Butter Fat Bombs to have in the freezer for a sweet nightcap; the recipe is on our blog, KetoConnect.net.

KEEP IT SIMPLE

Trying creative recipes that you find in cookbooks and on the internet is great, but you also want to have a handful of simple recipes that you make on a regular basis. Bacon and eggs, cobb salads, pan-roasted chicken thighs, and lettuce-wrapped burgers are the meals we make multiple times a week. We supplement those staples with more innovative recipes for date nights, movie nights, or on weekends when we have more time to cook. When you keep things simple, it's a lot easier to stay accountable and look at food more as a fuel source in which you take pleasure than as your reason for existing. We know that feeling all too well from our pre-keto days, and we've found that a keto diet comprised of simple yet filling meals has changed our overall relationship with food. Now, we crave the foods that make us feel the best!

FIND A PARTNER

Find a partner who will hold you accountable, and maybe even do the keto diet with you! It could be your significant other, your friend, your neighbor, or even your child. Luckily, we have each other, and it has proven to be a huge part of our success. We push each other to improve a little each day on our diets and in the gym. And if either of us has a slipup, we lend each other a hand of motivation, because there is always something to learn from a setback.

If you find that you aren't getting the support you need at home, you can look to social media support groups, such as those on Facebook and Instagram, to fill your needs. These are great places to share your struggles, stay accountable, and learn new tips and recipes.

HAVE A STRONG "WHY"

Ask yourself: Why are you doing this? Why are you making a change to your diet and a commitment to improve your health? For us, it was because we wanted more out of life. We were tired of getting home from work with barely enough energy to make it to the couch and watch TV for the rest of the night. Now, we've not only started a business but have written a cookbook, too! Figuring out your "why" is sometimes the easy part; it's reminding yourself that the "why" continues to exist and is your personal source of motivation and power, even on bad days, that is the hard part. We find that taking a moment each day, right when we wake up or just before bed, to reflect on our "why" helps us stay present and focused on what is most important to us. Doing this with your partner or in a support group is another great way to remember why you started this journey.

EAT ALL THE FAT

Eating a lot of fat is the trickiest part for most people who are just starting a keto diet. All our lives we've been taught that dietary fat is bad for us. We've been told that fat leads to high cholesterol, which leads to clogged arteries and ultimately heart attacks. But with each passing day, more information is revealed about how fat can play a vital role in our health and functionality. We know how hard it can be to make the switch to eating high-fat because we are former high-carb, low-fat eaters ourselves. We didn't let fear stop us from making the change, and neither should you!

Once you're able to grasp the high-fat concept—and we believe it'll become easier once you start eating a keto diet—things will seem more doable. You can start by switching from lean cuts of meat to fattier cuts and topping your salads with olive oil instead of low-fat dressings. Lots of little changes can make it easy to increase your daily fat intake. And remember, you don't have to be perfect. You're in this for the long haul, so if you find it hard to get in all your fats today, just try again tomorrow!

START PAYING ATTENTION

Before starting a keto diet, we never realized how out-of-tune we were with our bodies. There was such a disconnect between our food and how it made us feel. Then we started taking out carbs and, lo and behold, no two o'clock crash! That's when it clicked: the foods we eat have a huge impact on the way we feel.

Just because a food is keto-friendly or fits into your daily macros doesn't necessarily mean that it agrees with your body. A lot of people have dairy and nut intolerances but choose to eat those foods anyway. This could mean discomfort and bloating throughout the day, and who wants to live like that? By paying attention to what you put into your body and maybe even keeping track of what you've eaten in a journal, you could spot a trend that you never knew existed. To make eating and life a lot more intuitive, you need to know which situations and foods make you feel your best. A healthy inside leads to a healthy outside!

BEND, DON'T BREAK

We've all done it before: dived into a super strict diet for a few weeks before having a bad day, giving up on it, and indulging in all the foods we'd been deprived of. Let's take a different approach this time. Give in to a craving every once in a while so that you don't feel too restricted; just keep it keto. That way, you can make this diet a more sustainable lifestyle. Craving chocolate cheesecake? Head to page 210. What about chewy chocolate chip cookies? We've got those, too, on page 222. We want you to have options, and we want you to know that there is always a healthier substitute for whatever you're craving. This is why we've dedicated a whole chapter of this cookbook to decadent desserts!

Eating out or at events can be tough at first, too, but it's totally doable. Don't be scared to ask for substitutions, say no, or, if you feel guilty about saying no, kindly accept something and then set it down on the table. This is a time when your "why" comes into play. Why did you start this journey, and why do you want to stay on track?

DO YOUR RESEARCH

The keto diet is trendy right now, and for good reason. While it's tempting to jump in on a hot trend, we think it's important to do some research to get an understanding of the mechanisms behind the efficacy of the keto diet. Having a good base of knowledge will make it easier to stick to this way of eating when you're tempted to stray.

A lot of people ask us what differentiates keto from other low-carb diets, such as Atkins. Most of the differences are subtle, but one huge advantage sets keto apart from all the rest: keto puts your body in a metabolic state in which it uses ketones rather than glucose for fuel. Some of the benefits of being in ketosis are heightened energy, reduced appetite, and greater mental clarity, which is what makes keto more sustainable than any other low-carb diet. You won't feel restricted, and you won't feel low on energy. Your body will be using an entirely new fuel source and will begin functioning more efficiently than ever.

If you've never tracked your macros before, familiarizing yourself with the macronutrient makeup of common keto foods, such as eggs, avocado, butter, and bacon, could be a great idea. Knowing that nuts can be very calorie dense and can lead to a higher carb intake could make it easier for you to control portions, for example. Everyone's personal version of keto is going to look a little different, so doing your research and experimenting to find the foods you enjoy and make you feel good is the best way to get a head start! The books and websites that we've included in the "Suggested Reading" section on page 279 are a great place to start.

DON'T LET THE NUMBERS BOG YOU DOWN

A lot of people look to keto for weight loss, and justifiably so. When you deplete your body of carbohydrates, you naturally hold less water, hence you experience a sudden drop in weight. Although weight loss is a good reason to get healthy, keto has a lot of other benefits, such as heightened energy and focus. So don't let the numbers bog you down.

We are big proponents of relying on intuition. When you wake up, ask yourself how you feel. Do you feel great? If the answer is yes, then we honestly don't see a need to jump on the scale or test your blood. Yes, we all look for reassurance, but more often than not the scale can have a negative impact on mental health. It is important to know that your weight fluctuates from day to day, and it is impossible to gain 2 pounds of fat overnight. That being said, if you step on the scale and your weight is up a little—or even down, but not as low as you'd hoped—it may be time to put the scale away. The endgame is to feel good every day, have control over your eating, and enjoy life, so doesn't it seem a bit unfair to let a number on a scale dictate your happiness? We recommend working on mastering each day, focusing more on your daily actions than on the results.

Recipes

WAKE-UP CALL

PROTEIN WAFFLES

MAKES: 3 medium-sized waffles (1 per serving)   **PREP TIME:** 5 minutes   **COOK TIME:** 13 minutes

As a "bro" in recovery, Matt is always asking me to make him recipes using protein powder. He loves having these waffles with a cup of coffee after an early-morning workout.

WAFFLES:

4 large eggs

¼ cup natural peanut butter

¼ cup mascarpone cheese

¼ cup unsweetened almond milk

1 scoop unflavored whey protein powder

2 tablespoons unsalted butter, melted

TOPPINGS (OPTIONAL):

Sugar-free maple syrup

Natural peanut butter

Whipped cream

1. Preheat a waffle iron on the medium setting.

2. Put all the waffle ingredients in a large mixing bowl and combine using a whisk or an electric hand mixer.

3. Open the waffle iron and grease the top and bottom with coconut oil spray.

4. Using a ½-cup measuring cup, scoop up some of the batter and pour it into the center of the waffle iron. Close the lid and allow the waffle to cook for 4 to 4½ minutes, until golden brown.

5. Repeat with the remaining batter, making a total of 3 waffles.

6. Serve the waffles with maple syrup, peanut butter, and/or whipped cream, if desired.

TWIST

Matt loves to use these waffles to make a breakfast sandwich!

CALORIES: 409   FAT: 32.7g   PROTEIN: 24.3g   CARBS: 5.3g   FIBER: 2g

THREE-CHEESE SPINACH FRITTATA

MAKES: one 12-inch frittata (4 servings)   PREP TIME: 10 minutes   COOK TIME: 40 minutes

Two years ago, when we first started the keto diet, we ate a frittata for breakfast every morning. Needless to say, we got pretty good at making them. We usually have a few slices as soon as it comes out of the oven and save the rest for quick meals throughout the week.

8 large eggs

¼ cup heavy whipping cream

¼ cup water

⅓ cup shredded cheddar cheese, plus extra for the top (optional)

⅓ cup shredded Gruyère cheese, plus extra for the top (optional)

⅓ cup shredded fontina cheese, plus extra for the top (optional)

½ teaspoon garlic powder

¾ teaspoon pink Himalayan salt

¼ teaspoon ground black pepper

1 (10-ounce) package frozen spinach, thawed and drained

1. Preheat the oven to 350°F and grease a 12-inch cast-iron skillet with coconut oil spray.

2. Put the eggs, cream, and water in a large mixing bowl and whisk to combine. Add the three cheeses and seasonings and whisk together.

3. Pour the egg mixture into the greased skillet. Add the spinach, distributing it evenly throughout the skillet. Top with additional shredded cheese, if desired.

4. Bake for 35 to 40 minutes, until set in the center and lightly browned on the top. Allow to cool slightly before slicing and serving.

CALORIES: 148   FAT: 10.6g   PROTEIN: 10.4g   CARBS: 1.4g   FIBER: 0g

SAVORY ZUCCHINI CHEDDAR WAFFLES

MAKES: 4 medium-sized waffles (2 per serving)   **PREP TIME:** 10 minutes   **COOK TIME:** 18 minutes

Aside from caring for her pets and eating peanut butter straight from the jar, Megha's greatest passion is hiding vegetables in delicious baked goods. These zucchini cheddar waffles are a testament to that. They are tasty on their own but can also be used for sandwiches.

WAFFLES:

2 large zucchini

2 large eggs

²/₃ cup shredded cheddar cheese (about 2²/₃ ounces)

2 tablespoons coconut flour

½ teaspoon garlic powder

½ teaspoon red pepper flakes

¼ teaspoon pink Himalayan salt

FOR GARNISH (OPTIONAL):

Sour cream

Shredded cheddar cheese

Minced fresh chives

1. Preheat a waffle iron on the medium setting.

2. Using a vegetable or cheese grater, grate the zucchini into a large colander set inside of a bowl. Squeeze the excess water out of the grated zucchini using your hands and drain.

3. Add the eggs and cheese to the drained zucchini and combine with a fork. Add the coconut flour, garlic powder, red pepper flakes, and salt and use the fork to combine once more.

4. Open the waffle iron and grease the top and bottom with coconut oil spray.

5. Using a ⅓-cup measuring cup, scoop out some of the batter, place it in the center of the waffle iron, and close the lid. Cook the waffle for 4 to 4½ minutes, until golden brown and fully cooked through. Use a fork to lift it off the iron and set on a plate.

6. Repeat with the remaining batter, making a total of 4 waffles. Garnish with sour cream, shredded cheddar cheese, and/or minced chives, if desired.

CALORIES: 292   FAT: 19g   PROTEIN: 20g   CARBS: 14g   FIBER: 5g

FIVE-STAR BREAKFAST SANDWICH 👍

MAKES: 1 serving

PREP TIME: 10 minutes (not including time to make bread) **COOK TIME:** 8 minutes

It might sound odd, but Matt's all-time favorite food is a breakfast sandwich. What sets this one apart is the Parmesan cheese–crusted sandwich bread. It's a little bit of extra work, but it's well worth it!

1 large egg

2 slices The Best Keto Bread (page 76)

2 tablespoons grated Parmesan cheese

1 slice cheddar cheese

1 slice fontina cheese

1 slice bacon, cooked until crispy

3 slices avocado

1. Heat a small skillet over medium-high heat and grease the surface with coconut oil spray.

2. When the skillet is hot, crack in the egg and cover the pan with a lid. Cook until the white is cooked through and the yolk is cooked to your liking. Remove the egg from the skillet and set aside.

3. Preheat the oven broiler to high.

4. Spray one side of each slice of keto bread with coconut oil spray, then evenly sprinkle the Parmesan on the sides sprayed with oil. Press the cheese into the bread with your hands, if needed.

5. Put the bread in the hot skillet, cheese side down. Cook for 2 minutes, or until the cheese has browned and hardened. Remove from the skillet and set one slice, cheese side down, on an oven-safe plate.

6. Layer the cheddar and fontina cheeses on the bread. Cut the bacon in half and layer on top of the cheese. Place in the oven and broil for 2 to 3 minutes, until the cheese has melted.

7. Remove from the oven and layer with the cooked egg, avocado slices, and second slice of bread, putting the Parmesan-crusted side face up.

CALORIES: 585   FAT: 39.8g   PROTEIN: 28.6g   CARBS: 5.4g   FIBER: 3.1g

CHORIZO COTIJA MORNING MUFFINS

MAKES: 1 dozen muffins (1 per serving)   **PREP TIME:** 15 minutes   **COOK TIME:** 27 minutes

Having these flavorful high-fat, high-fiber muffins to keep you satisfied between meals can be hugely beneficial when first switching to a ketogenic diet.

6 ounces fresh (raw) chorizo

½ cup (1 stick) unsalted butter, melted (but not hot)

4 large eggs

¼ cup water

1 cup golden flax meal

¼ cup coconut flour

1 cup shredded Cotija cheese (about 4 ounces), plus extra for garnish (optional)

1 teaspoon baking powder

½ teaspoon pink Himalayan salt

½ teaspoon garlic powder

½ teaspoon dried oregano leaves

¼ teaspoon chili powder

¼ teaspoon paprika

1. Preheat the oven to 350°F and line a standard-size 12-well muffin tin with paper liners.

2. Heat a medium-sized skillet over medium-high heat. Slice open the chorizo links and squeeze the sausage into the hot skillet. Using a spatula, flatten and break apart the sausage. Cook for 5 to 7 minutes, until cooked through. Remove the chorizo from the skillet and set aside on a paper towel–lined plate.

3. Put the melted butter, eggs, and water in a large bowl and combine using a whisk. Add the flax meal, coconut flour, Cotija cheese, baking powder, and seasonings and combine with a rubber spatula.

4. Add the cooked chorizo and stir to combine. Using a cookie scoop or spoon, scoop the mixture evenly into the 12 cupcake liners, filling them nearly to the top.

5. Bake for 20 minutes, or until a toothpick inserted in the center of a muffin comes out clean. Allow to cool in the pan for at least 10 minutes before removing and serving. Garnish with extra Cotija, if desired.

6. Store leftovers in a sealed container or zip-top plastic bag for up to a week. To reheat, microwave for 30 to 45 seconds. Unfortunately, these muffins do not freeze well.

CALORIES: 246   FAT: 19.6g   PROTEIN: 12.4g   CARBS: 5.4g   FIBER: 3.5g

BREAKFAST COOKIES

MAKES: 6 cookies (1 per serving)   **PREP TIME:** 10 minutes   **COOK TIME:** 15 minutes

We love to have a grab-and-go breakfast ready for busy days. These high-fat, high-fiber breakfast cookies are the perfect way to start your morning. The addition of cacao nibs gives them a nice chocolaty crunch.

⅔ cup flax meal

2 teaspoons ground cinnamon

½ cup natural peanut butter

¼ cup sugar-free maple syrup

¼ cup unsweetened almond milk

¼ cup cacao nibs

Special equipment:

6-cavity, 3½-inch-diameter silicone muffin top pan

1. Preheat the oven to 300°F and grease a 6-cavity, 3½-inch-diameter silicone muffin top pan.

2. Put the flax meal and cinnamon in a medium-sized mixing bowl and blend with a fork. Add the peanut butter, maple syrup, and almond milk and stir to combine.

3. Using a rubber spatula, fold in the cacao nibs. Scoop the batter evenly into the muffin top pan, filling each cavity to the brim.

4. Bake for 15 minutes, or until the cookies are firm. Allow to cool in the molds for 20 minutes before handling and serving.

5. Store leftovers in a sealed container or zip-top plastic bag for up to a week. The cookies can be frozen for up to 3 weeks and are best reheated in a 250°F oven for 10 minutes.

CALORIES: 225   FAT: 17.5g   PROTEIN: 8.7g   CARBS: 12g   FIBER: 7.5g   SUGAR ALCOHOL: 0.8g

OVERNIGHT PROTEIN OATS

MAKES: 1 serving **ACTIVE PREP TIME:** 5 minutes **INACTIVE PREP TIME:** at least 4 hours

We are fans of anything that can be made in a mason jar. This keto oatmeal is loaded with hemp hearts and chia seeds and packs over 20 grams of protein. Letting it sit overnight allows the chia seeds to naturally thicken the oatmeal.

¼ cup heavy whipping cream

3 tablespoons hemp hearts

1 tablespoon chia seeds

1 scoop flavored protein powder of choice

1. Put all the ingredients in a bowl and stir to combine. Cover with plastic wrap and place in the refrigerator for at least 4 hours or overnight.

2. Serve cold, straight out of the refrigerator, or microwave on high for 20 to 30 seconds before serving.

NOTE

If you use unflavored protein powder, you can add 7 to 10 drops of liquid stevia to replace the sweetener found in flavored protein powder.

CALORIES: 439   **FAT:** 28g   **PROTEIN:** 39g   **CARBS:** 9g   **FIBER:** 8g

BREAKFAST ROLL-UPS

MAKES: 3 roll-ups (1 per serving)   **PREP TIME:** 5 minutes   **COOK TIME:** 11 minutes

How do you make a breakfast wrap without a tortilla? You use an egg! You can stuff these egg wraps with any fillings you'd like, but our favorite is this tasty combination of spinach, bacon, and goat cheese.

4 large eggs

¼ cup heavy whipping cream

½ teaspoon pink Himalayan salt

6 ounces fresh spinach

6 slices bacon, cooked

2 ounces fresh (soft) goat cheese

1. Heat a 12-inch skillet over low heat and grease with coconut oil spray.

2. Put the eggs, cream, and salt in a medium-sized bowl and whisk to combine.

3. Using a ⅓-cup measuring cup, scoop out some of the egg mixture and place it in the center of the hot skillet. Tilt the pan so that the mixture coats the entire flat surface. Cover with a lid and cook for 2 to 3 minutes, until cooked through. Repeat with the rest of the egg mixture to make a total of 3 egg wraps.

4. Turn the heat up to medium-high, grease the skillet with coconut oil spray, and add the spinach. Cover with the lid and cook for 1 to 2 minutes, until the spinach has wilted and cooked down. Remove from the skillet.

5. Divide the cooked spinach among the 3 egg wraps, placing it along the edge of each wrap. Place 2 slices of bacon on top of the spinach in each wrap and divide the goat cheese evenly among the wraps.

6. Starting at the edge with the fillings, roll each egg wrap into a burrito, folding in the ends, or simply roll it up like crepe. Serve warm.

TWIST

Matt also likes to fill his roll-up with avocado and Sriracha sauce for a spicy start to his day!

CALORIES: 299   **FAT:** 23.7g   **PROTEIN:** 20.3g   **CARBS:** 4.3g   **FIBER:** 1.7g

EASY EGGS BENEDICT

MAKES: 1 serving **PREP TIME:** 10 minutes (not including time to make English muffin)
COOK TIME: 15 minutes

This is one of those rare comfort foods that needs very few adjustments to make it keto-friendly. While you could just leave out the English muffin, we've never been the type to settle. Pop a tasty keto English muffin under this high-fat classic and enjoy!

HOLLANDAISE SAUCE:
(makes enough for 4 servings)

2 large egg yolks

½ cup (1 stick) unsalted butter, melted but not hot

1 teaspoon lemon juice

½ teaspoon distilled white vinegar

½ teaspoon pink Himalayan salt

2 large eggs

1 tablespoon distilled white vinegar

1 English Muffin (page 70)

2 slices Canadian bacon, cooked

1. Make the hollandaise: Put all the ingredients for the hollandaise in a tall, narrow cup that is wide enough to fit an immersion blender and blend until smooth. Set aside.

2. Poach the eggs: Fill a saucepan halfway full of water. Add the vinegar and bring to a simmer over medium heat.

3. Crack each egg into a small ramekin and set aside. Once the water reaches a simmer, use a spoon to quickly swirl the water in one direction until it's spinning like a whirlpool.

4. Drop an egg into the center of the whirlpool and cook for 3 to 5 minutes, until the white is fully cooked. Remove with a slotted spoon and immediately place in an ice bath. Repeat the process with the second egg.

5. To assemble, slice the muffin in half and toast in a toaster or in the oven. Lay the halves on a plate. Top each half with a slice of Canadian bacon and a poached egg. Drizzle on one-quarter of the hollandaise sauce. Serve immediately.

NOTES

We have found that our one-step method of making hollandaise differs from most, but it's a quick way to whip up a delicious sauce on your busiest mornings. Feel free to improvise with your preferred method.

This recipe makes more hollandaise than you will need for one serving of Eggs Benedict. Store leftover sauce in a sealed container in the refrigerator for up to 3 days. Reheat in the microwave for 30 to 45 seconds or in a saucepan on the stovetop over medium-low heat.

CALORIES: 651   **FAT:** 54.8g   **PROTEIN:** 26.3g   **CARBS:** 14.4g   **FIBER:** 9.5g

GOLDEN GATE GRANOLA

MAKES: 4 cups (¼ cup per serving) **ACTIVE PREP TIME:** 10 minutes
INACTIVE PREP TIME: 1 hour **COOK TIME:** 1 hour

Whenever we go on a weekend trip, we always make a big batch of granola.
It's a perfect quick snack that you can feel good about.

¼ cup (½ stick) unsalted butter

¼ cup powdered erythritol

¼ teaspoon plus 10 drops of liquid stevia

1 teaspoon ground cinnamon

½ teaspoon vanilla extract

1 cup raw almonds

1 cup raw hazelnuts

1 cup unsweetened coconut flakes

½ cup raw pumpkin seeds

¼ cup hemp hearts

1. Preheat the oven to 275°F and line a rimmed baking sheet with parchment paper or a silicone baking mat.

2. In a small saucepan over medium heat, combine the butter, erythritol, stevia, cinnamon, and vanilla extract. Stirring occasionally, heat until the butter and erythritol are melted and dissolved. Remove from the heat and set aside.

3. In a large bowl, combine the nuts, coconut flakes, pumpkin seeds, and hemp hearts. Pour the melted butter mixture over the nut mixture and toss using a rubber spatula, making sure that everything is well coated.

4. Pour the granola onto the lined baking sheet and spread it out into an even layer. Bake for 1 hour, stirring every 15 minutes or so, until dark golden brown.

5. Let the granola cool in the pan for at least 1 hour to allow it to harden and form clumps. Store in a sealed jar or zip-top plastic bag for up to 3 weeks. It does not need to be refrigerated.

TIP

This is a great snack for whenever you're on the go. Make it for your kids, for your next road trip, or just to keep at your desk or in your purse for times when you need a snack!

CALORIES: 200 FAT: 18.1g PROTEIN: 4.9g CARBS: 5.4g FIBER: 3.3g SUGAR ALCOHOL: 3g

SAUSAGE AND GRUYÈRE BREAKFAST CASSEROLE

MAKES: 8 servings **PREP TIME:** 15 minutes **COOK TIME:** 50 minutes

Breakfast can get boring, especially when eggs are often on the menu. We quickly learned that breakfast casseroles make great use of eggs while transforming them into something exciting and delicious. Instead of using store-bought bulk breakfast sausage, we season fresh ground pork with spices and fresh herbs. Add eggs, cream, and Gruyère, and you have a hearty and filling breakfast casserole dish! Make it on the weekends for brunch or to enjoy on weekday mornings before you head off to work.

¾ pound unseasoned ground pork

1 bunch scallions, chopped

½ teaspoon red pepper flakes

Pinch of ground cloves

1 teaspoon pink Himalayan salt

¼ teaspoon ground black pepper

1 tablespoon chopped fresh sage

1 teaspoon chopped fresh marjoram

8 large eggs

¼ cup heavy whipping cream

1¼ cups shredded Gruyère cheese (about 5 ounces), divided

1. Preheat the oven to 350°F and grease a 1¾-quart baking dish with coconut oil spray.

2. In a large skillet over medium-high heat, partially cook the pork, stirring to break it up, about 5 minutes. Add the scallions, red pepper flakes, cloves, salt, and pepper and stir to combine. Continue to cook until the pork is fully cooked and browned, an additional 5 minutes.

3. Add the sage and marjoram and stir to combine—now you have your own seasoned breakfast sausage! Pour the cooked sausage into the greased baking dish.

4. In a bowl, whisk together the eggs, cream, and 1 cup of the shredded cheese. Pour over the sausage in the casserole dish.

5. Sprinkle the remaining Gruyère over the top of the casserole and bake for 40 minutes, or until the eggs are fully set in the center and the top is golden brown.

NOTE

You can stir the sausage and egg mixture before baking it if you want an even distribution of all the ingredients.

CALORIES: 282   FAT: 22g   PROTEIN: 18.6g   CARBS: 1.1g   FIBER: 0g

DINER PANCAKES

OPTION

MAKES: eight 5- to 6-inch pancakes (2 per serving)   **PREP TIME:** 10 minutes
COOK TIME: 28 minutes

This is your classic diner pancake in low-carb form! The combination of coconut flour and golden flax meal gives these pancakes just the right amount of fluff and texture, along with a great flavor to bring you back to your childhood days of Sunday brunch. We like to top them with butter and sugar-free maple syrup.

¼ cup plus 2 tablespoons coconut flour

¼ cup finely ground golden flax meal

1 teaspoon baking powder

¼ teaspoon pink Himalayan salt

¼ cup (½ stick) unsalted butter, melted but not hot

½ teaspoon vanilla extract

15 drops of liquid stevia

6 large eggs

¾ cup unsweetened coconut milk or almond milk

FOR SERVING:

Butter

Sugar-free maple syrup

1. In a small mixing bowl, whisk together the coconut flour, flax meal, baking powder, and salt. Set aside.

2. Put the melted butter, vanilla extract, and stevia in a large mixing bowl. While whisking, add the eggs one at a time. Continue whisking for 60 to 90 seconds, until the mixture is airy and fully combined.

3. Add the milk to the egg mixture and whisk to combine.

4. Add the dry ingredients to the wet ingredients in 2 batches, whisking until fully combined. Allow the batter to sit for 5 minutes before cooking.

5. Heat a nonstick skillet over medium-low heat. Grease the pan with coconut oil spray.

6. Using a ¼-cup measuring cup, scoop up some of the batter and pour it into the center of the skillet. If the batter does not spread out on its own, use a spoon to spread it out until it is 5 to 6 inches in diameter. (*Note:* You can make the pancakes any size you want; just keep in mind that changing the size will affect the yield and possibly the cooking time.) The pancake is ready to flip when bubbles start to form on the surface, about 3 minutes. Flip and cook for another minute, until golden brown on both sides.

7. Repeat this process with the remaining batter, making a total of 8 pancakes. Grease the pan after each pancake. To keep the pancakes warm while the rest are cooking, place them on a baking sheet in a 200°F oven.

8. Serve the pancakes warm with butter and sugar-free maple syrup.

CALORIES: 298   FAT: 23.5g   PROTEIN: 12.5g   CARBS: 8.8g   FIBER: 5.5g

TWIST

Add some sugar-free chocolate chips or a handful of berries for a fun take on this classic recipe.

9. Allow to cool before storing in a sealed container in the refrigerator for up to 5 days. Reheat in a preheated 200°F oven for 15 minutes or in the microwave for 30 seconds. Sadly, these pancakes do not freeze well.

NOTES

The ideal texture of the flax meal for this recipe is very finely ground. It should be powdery and almost as fine as flour. If the flax meal you have at home is not finely ground, pulse it in a coffee grinder until it's very fine. **The finer the flax meal, the fluffier your pancakes will be.**

To make these pancakes nut-free, use coconut milk.

TOASTED OATMEAL

OPTION

MAKES: roughly 3 cups (½ cup per serving)   **ACTIVE PREP TIME:** 7 minutes
INACTIVE PREP TIME: 30 minutes

Sadly, oatmeal made with oats is the furthest thing from keto-friendly, and we miss it just as much as you probably do! So we created the perfect combination of chia seeds, toasted coconut flakes, and nuts to create a low-carb version of oatmeal that some even say is better than the real thing! This is our favorite make-ahead breakfast when we know we have a busy week coming up or just simply want a change from good old bacon and eggs!

¼ cup raw almonds

¼ cup raw pecans

½ cup unsweetened coconut flakes

½ cup heavy whipping cream or coconut cream (see page 23)

¼ cup chia seeds

¾ cup water

1 teaspoon ground cinnamon

½ teaspoon vanilla extract

¼ teaspoon maple extract (optional)

15 drops of liquid stevia

1. Finely chop the nuts.

2. Toast the nuts and coconut flakes in a medium-sized nonstick skillet over low heat, stirring continuously, for about 5 minutes, until fragrant and lightly golden. Pour the toasted nuts and coconut flakes into a large mixing bowl.

3. Add the rest of the ingredients to the mixing bowl and gently stir everything together. Refrigerate for 30 minutes to allow the chia seeds to expand and the oatmeal to thicken prior to serving.

4. Serve the oatmeal straight out of the refrigerator or microwave for 1 minute and serve warm. We prefer it warm!

5. Store in a sealed mason jar or other container in the refrigerator for up to a week.

NOTES

Any kind of nuts can be used in this recipe. The maple extract is optional, but it greatly adds to the flavor, and we do not advise leaving it out! The sweetness can easily be changed by adjusting the amount of stevia you add.

To make this oatmeal dairy-free, use coconut cream instead of heavy whipping cream.

CALORIES: 266   FAT: 24.8g   PROTEIN: 5.2g   CARBS: 9.6g   FIBER: 5.8g

ICED BULLETPROOF COFFEE FRAPPÉ

MAKES: 1 serving   **PREP TIME:** 5 minutes   **COOK TIME:** 1 minute

We love starting our days with a frothy cup of bulletproof coffee. However, on warm summer mornings, we sometimes want those same healthy fats in a cool and refreshing iced coffee, pureed to smooth, creamy perfection in a blender.

8 ounces brewed coffee, cold

1 tablespoon heavy whipping cream

1 tablespoon MCT oil

1 scoop unflavored collagen peptides

15 drops of liquid stevia

¼ teaspoon ground cinnamon

¼ teaspoon xanthan gum

6 or 7 ice cubes

TOPPINGS (OPTIONAL):

Whipped cream

Ground cinnamon

Place all the ingredients in a blender and blend until smooth. Pour into a 16-ounce glass and top with whipped cream and cinnamon, if desired.

NOTES

If you are new to using MCT oil, you may want to start with 1 teaspoon and work your way up to 1 tablespoon because it can cause digestive issues and discomfort. You can also replace the MCT oil with 2 tablespoons of heavy whipping cream, which will decrease the fat by 4 grams and increase the carbs by 1 gram.

CALORIES: 220   FAT: 20g   PROTEIN: 10g   CARBS: 0.3g   FIBER: 0.1g

MOCHA PROTEIN KEThe COFFEE

MOCHA PROTEIN KETO COFFEE

MAKES: 1 serving   **PREP TIME:** 5 minutes   **COOK TIME:** 1 minute

We live for our morning coffees. We make it a point to spend time with our cat, Miley, and our dog, Julius, every morning while we drink our coffee. On days when we have to rush out of the house, we make this coffee as a meal replacement. Not only is it delicious, but it has the fat and protein we need to power us through the day.

12 ounces hot brewed coffee

2 tablespoons heavy whipping cream

1 tablespoon unsalted butter

1 tablespoon cocoa powder

1 scoop chocolate-flavored protein powder

1 scoop unflavored collagen peptides

10 drops of liquid stevia

Place all the ingredients in a blender and blend until smooth and frothy. Pour into a 16-ounce mug and serve immediately, or pour it into a Thermos and take it on the go!

TWIST

Megha likes to change up the protein powder to alter the flavor of her coffee. Her favorite is Isopure's cookies and cream flavor, which turns this into a cookies and cream protein coffee!

CALORIES: 361   FAT: 24g   PROTEIN: 37g   CARBS: 4g   FIBER: 2g

FRESH BAKED

ENGLISH MUFFINS

MAKES: 8 muffins (1 per serving)   **PREP TIME:** 10 minutes   **COOK TIME:** 50 minutes

True story: Matt used to make homemade English muffins every weekend when he was away at college, so it was only a matter of time before we figured out how to make a good keto version. We love using these for egg sandwiches or toasting and spreading them with peanut butter.

½ cup psyllium husk powder

½ cup coconut flour

2 teaspoons baking powder

1 tablespoon active dry yeast (optional, for flavor)

8 large eggs

½ cup avocado oil

Butter, for serving

TIP

Our favorite way to eat these is to cut an English muffin in half, spread butter on each cut side, and toast butter side down in a nonstick skillet for 2 to 3 minutes, until browned.

1. Preheat the oven to 300°F.

2. Put the psyllium husk powder, coconut flour, and baking powder in a medium-sized bowl and mix well with a fork. If desired, add the yeast for flavor and whisk to combine.

3. Put the eggs and oil in a large bowl and combine with a hand mixer. Add the dry ingredients in 2 parts and combine with the hand mixer after each addition. Allow the dough to rest for 5 minutes.

4. While the dough is resting, heat a 12-inch cast-iron skillet over medium heat and grease with coconut oil spray.

5. Using your hands, form the dough into 8 round English muffin shapes, about 3 inches in diameter and ½ inch thick. If the dough is not able to be formed by hand, slowly add up to 3 tablespoons more coconut flour until the dough is easy to shape. Because coconut flour is highly absorptive, it is important to add a little at a time, mix, and then judge the consistency before adding more.

6. Place half of the English muffins in the hot skillet and cook for 5 minutes on each side, or until golden brown. Remove the muffins from the pan and set aside. Repeat with the remaining half of the muffins, then return the muffins you set aside to the pan.

7. Transfer the skillet to the oven and bake the muffins for 15 minutes, until browned and firm to touch. Transfer the muffins to a plate or wire baking rack and let cool for 10 minutes before serving.

8. Store leftovers in the refrigerator for up to a week or freeze for up to a month.

CALORIES: 251   **FAT:** 19.8g   **PROTEIN:** 7.3g   **CARBS:** 12.4g   **FIBER:** 9.5g

CHEDDAR AND THYME CORNBREAD

MAKES: one 8-inch round loaf (8 servings)   **PREP TIME:** 15 minutes   **COOK TIME:** 25 minutes

Is there anything better than a thick slice of cornbread? The secret ingredient in this version is baby corn. Baby corn is very low in carbs and has a subtle corn flavor, but it greatly adds to the texture of this keto cornbread.

¾ cup baby corn

1½ cups blanched almond flour

1 tablespoon dried thyme leaves

1 tablespoon baking powder

¼ teaspoon cream of tartar

¼ teaspoon pink Himalayan salt

4 large eggs, room temperature

10 drops of liquid stevia

¼ cup (½ stick) unsalted butter, melted but not hot

⅔ cup shredded cheddar cheese (about 2⅔ ounces)

TWIST

Matt likes to fold in minced jalapeño peppers for a spicy cheese cornbread.

1. Preheat the oven to 375°F and grease an 8-inch round cake pan with coconut oil spray.

2. Put the baby corn in a food processor and lightly pulse until the corn is chopped but still chunky; do not puree. Set aside.

3. Put the almond flour, thyme, baking powder, cream of tartar, and salt in a medium-sized bowl and mix well with a fork.

4. Put the eggs and stevia in a large mixing bowl and beat with a hand mixer until combined. With the mixer running, slowly pour in the melted butter, continuing to mix until all the butter is added.

5. Add half of the almond flour mixture to the egg mixture and mix to combine. Add the second half and continue mixing until all the clumps are gone.

6. Fold the cheddar cheese and baby corn into the batter with a rubber spatula.

7. Pour the batter into the greased cake pan and smooth the top. Bake for 25 minutes, until a toothpick comes out clean when inserted in the center. Allow to cool in the pan for 15 minutes, then cut into 8 slices.

8. Store leftovers in the refrigerator for up to a week.

CALORIES: 249   **FAT:** 21.4g   **PROTEIN:** 10.6g   **CARBS:** 5.8g   **FIBER:** 2.9g

MICROWAVE BREAD

MAKES: 1 serving   **PREP TIME:** 2 to 3 minutes   **COOK TIME:** about 1½ minutes

You've got all the fixings for a tasty sandwich in the fridge, but you're missing the bread? Whip up this microwave bread in under five minutes and you won't be disappointed!

1 tablespoon unsalted butter

1½ tablespoons blanched almond flour

1½ tablespoons golden flax meal

1 large egg

½ teaspoon baking powder

1. Put the butter in a wide 12-ounce coffee cup or microwave-safe ramekin. Microwave on high for 20 to 30 seconds, until the butter is melted.

2. Add the remaining ingredients to the melted butter and mix with a fork. Microwave on high for 60 to 70 seconds, until the bread is cooked through and set in the center.

3. Allow to cool in the mug for 2 to 3 minutes, then run a knife around the edge to release the bread. Slice in half and enjoy.

TWIST

Matt never waits for his bread to cool because hot bread is optimal for smothering in peanut butter!

CALORIES: 285   FAT: 25g   PROTEIN: 10g   CARBS: 6g   FIBER: 4g

THE BEST KETO BREAD

MAKES: one 8 by 4-inch loaf (16 servings)   PREP TIME: 10 minutes   COOK TIME: 30 minutes

This is by far the most popular recipe on our blog. Thousands of people have made this bread. When we started writing this cookbook, it was the first recipe we decided to include. It's the perfect combination of simplicity and quality taste.

6 large eggs

¼ teaspoon cream of tartar

1½ cups blanched almond flour

¼ cup (½ stick) unsalted butter, melted but not hot

1 tablespoon baking powder

½ teaspoon pink Himalayan salt

10 drops of liquid stevia

1. Preheat the oven to 375°F and grease an 8 by 4-inch loaf pan with coconut oil spray.

2. Separate the eggs. Put the whites and cream of tartar in a large mixing bowl and beat with a hand mixer on high speed until stiff peaks form.

3. Put the egg yolks, almond flour, melted butter, baking powder, salt, stevia, and one-third of the beaten egg whites in another large mixing bowl. Mix with the hand mixer until you have a thick, uniform dough.

4. Using a rubber spatula, fold in the remaining whipped egg whites in 2 parts.

5. Pour the batter into the greased loaf pan and bake for 30 minutes, until the bread is set in the center and a toothpick inserted in the center comes out clean. Allow to cool in the pan for 10 minutes before removing and slicing.

6. Store leftovers in a zip-top plastic bag for up to 5 days or freeze for up to 2 weeks. It is best reheated in the oven.

CALORIES: 112   FAT: 9.8g   PROTEIN: 4.6g   CARBS: 2.4g   FIBER: 1.1g

RASPBERRY FIBER MUFFINS

MAKES: 1 dozen muffins (1 per serving)   PREP TIME: 15 minutes   COOK TIME: 17 minutes

When Matt first learned that Megha's favorite type of muffin is a bran muffin, he made it his mission to come up with an awesome keto version, and this is it. We always bring these muffins with us on our weekend hikes.

1 cup flax meal

1 cup oat fiber

2 teaspoons ground cinnamon

1 teaspoon baking powder

½ teaspoon baking soda

½ teaspoon pink Himalayan salt

¼ cup (½ stick) unsalted butter

¼ cup granular erythritol

4 large eggs, room temperature

½ cup heavy whipping cream

½ teaspoon vanilla extract

½ cup fresh raspberries, divided

TWIST

Megha likes to warm her muffin, cut it in half, and top it with 1 tablespoon of butter to get her mornings off to a fibrous and fatty start!

1. Preheat the oven to 350°F. Line a standard-size 12-well muffin tin with paper liners, then spray the liners with coconut oil spray.

2. Put the flax meal, oat fiber, cinnamon, baking powder, baking soda, and salt in a medium-sized bowl and mix well with a fork. Set aside.

3. Put the butter in a large microwave-safe bowl and microwave on high for 30 seconds, or until melted. Add the erythritol and beat with a hand mixer until fully combined. Add the eggs, cream, and vanilla extract and mix with the hand mixer until fully combined.

4. Add the dry ingredients to the butter mixture and mix using a whisk until a thick batter forms.

5. Set aside 3 large raspberries for garnish, if desired. Using a rubber spatula, fold the rest of the raspberries into the batter.

6. Distribute the batter evenly among the muffin liners, filling them about three-quarters full. If you have set aside raspberries, cut each of the reserved berries into fourths and place a fourth on top of each muffin.

7. Bake for 15 to 17 minutes, until a toothpick inserted in the middle of a muffin comes out clean. Allow to cool in the pan for 15 minutes before removing and serving.

8. Store leftovers in the refrigerator for up to a week.

CALORIES: 131   FAT: 10.4g   PROTEIN: 4.2g   CARBS: 11g   FIBER: 9.8g   SUGAR ALCOHOL: 4g

CHEDDAR JALAPEÑO BAGELS

MAKES: 6 bagels (1 per serving) **PREP TIME:** 10 minutes **COOK TIME:** 18 minutes

For us, part of the fun of being keto is re-creating all our favorite foods in a healthier way. These bagels are the perfect example.

2 jalapeño peppers

3 scoops unflavored whey protein powder

1½ teaspoons baking powder

¾ teaspoon garlic powder

¾ teaspoon onion powder

½ teaspoon pink Himalayan salt

5 ounces cream cheese (10 tablespoons), room temperature

¼ cup (½ stick) unsalted butter, room temperature

1 large egg, room temperature

¾ cup shredded cheddar cheese (about 3 ounces), divided

Cream cheese, for serving (optional)

Special equipment:

6-well silicone donut pan

1. Preheat the oven to 350°F and grease a 6-well silicone donut pan with coconut oil spray.

2. Mince one of the jalapeño peppers and slice the other crosswise into rounds.

3. Put the protein powder, baking powder, garlic powder, onion powder, and salt in a medium-sized bowl and mix well with a fork.

4. Put the cream cheese, butter, and egg in a large bowl and cream with a hand mixer until there are no clumps. Add the dry ingredients and continue to mix with the hand mixer until a thick batter has formed.

5. Add ¼ cup of the shredded cheese and the minced jalapeño to the batter and fold in with a rubber spatula.

6. Evenly distribute the batter among the greased wells of the donut pan, filling them nearly to the top. Top with the remaining ½ cup of shredded cheese and the jalapeño slices. Bake for 18 minutes, or until a toothpick inserted in the center of a bagel comes out clean.

7. Allow to cool in the pan for 10 minutes before removing. To serve, slice in half and spread with cream cheese, if desired.

8. Store leftovers in the refrigerator for up to a week.

TWIST

Megha always makes sandwiches using these bagels, some sliced cooked chicken thighs, and a heaping dollop of guacamole!

CALORIES: 334   FAT: 25.5g   PROTEIN: 22.8g   CARBS: 2.8g   FIBER: 0.5g

LOW-CARB DINNER ROLLS

MAKES: 10 rolls (1 per serving)   PREP TIME: 15 minutes   COOK TIME: 35 minutes

If you've tried a bunch of different low-carb bread recipes and you haven't found anything with a true bread texture, then let us introduce you to your new favorite recipe. The combination of coconut flour and psyllium husk powder gives these rolls the doughy, fluffy consistency you've been looking for.

½ cup coconut flour

2 tablespoons psyllium husk powder

½ teaspoon baking powder

¼ teaspoon pink Himalayan salt

4 large eggs, room temperature

¾ cup water

¼ cup (½ stick) unsalted butter, melted but not hot

1. Preheat the oven to 350°F and line a baking sheet with parchment paper.

2. Put the coconut flour, psyllium husk powder, baking powder, and salt in a medium-sized bowl and mix well with a fork.

3. Put the eggs in a large bowl and beat with a hand mixer until combined and frothy on top. Add the water, then slowly add the melted butter while mixing with the hand mixer.

4. Add the dry ingredients to the wet ingredients in 2 parts, combining with the hand mixer after each addition.

5. Shape the dough by hand into 10 rolls, about 2 inches in diameter. If the dough is not shapeable, add more coconut flour a little bit at a time until the dough is easy to shape. Place on the lined baking sheet, about 3 inches apart, and bake for 30 to 35 minutes, until the rolls are firm and slightly browned on top. Allow to cool on the baking sheet for 10 minutes before serving.

6. Store leftovers in the refrigerator for up to a week.

CALORIES: 99   FAT: 7.1g   PROTEIN: 3.3g   CARBS: 4.9g   FIBER: 3.4g

CINNAMON WALNUT SCONES

MAKES: 8 scones (1 per serving) **PREP TIME:** 15 minutes **COOK TIME:** 40 minutes

A few years ago, you could often find either of us hovering around the pastry display case at the local coffee shop saying, "I'll start my diet tomorrow." These scones have single-handedly changed that!

¾ cup coconut flour

¼ cup plus 2 tablespoons granular erythritol

1 teaspoon ground cinnamon, plus extra for garnish (optional)

½ teaspoon baking powder

¼ teaspoon pink Himalayan salt

4 large eggs, room temperature

¼ cup extra-virgin olive oil

⅓ cup raw walnuts, chopped, plus extra for garnish (optional)

1. Preheat the oven to 350°F and line a baking sheet with parchment paper.

2. Put the coconut flour, erythritol, cinnamon, baking powder, and salt in a medium-sized bowl and mix well with a fork.

3. Put the eggs and olive oil in a large bowl and combine using a hand mixer. Add the dry ingredients in 2 parts, combining after each addition with the hand mixer.

4. Fold in the walnuts with a rubber spatula until they are evenly distributed.

5. Form the dough into a 1-inch-thick circle on the lined baking sheet. Cut into 8 wedges and separate slightly. If desired, garnish with additional chopped walnuts, gently pressing them into the dough.

6. Bake for 35 to 40 minutes, until the edges are lightly browned.

7. Remove from the oven and, if desired, dust with cinnamon. Allow to cool on the baking sheet for 10 minutes before serving.

8. Store leftovers in the refrigerator for up to a week.

CALORIES: 174   FAT: 14.0g   PROTEIN: 5.5g   CARBS: 7g   FIBER: 4.3g   SUGAR ALCOHOL: 9g

CHOCOLATE CHIP ZUCCHINI BREAD

MAKES: one 8 by 4-inch loaf (12 servings)   PREP TIME: 15 minutes   COOK TIME: 50 minutes

Baking with zucchini is great for a couple of reasons. Not only is it a good way to sneak some veggies into your diet, but it also makes breads incredibly moist.

1 loosely packed cup grated zucchini

6 large eggs, room temperature

½ cup extra-virgin olive oil

1 teaspoon vanilla extract

½ teaspoon liquid stevia

1 cup coconut flour

1 teaspoon baking powder

½ cup sugar-free chocolate chips

1. Preheat the oven to 350°F and line an 8 by 4-inch loaf pan with parchment paper, leaving some paper overhanging for easy removal of the bread.

2. Place the grated zucchini in a large bowl. Add the eggs, olive oil, vanilla extract, and stevia. Combine using a hand mixer.

3. Add the coconut flour and baking powder and combine with the hand mixer until the ingredients are fully incorporated and there are no clumps of batter remaining.

4. Using a rubber spatula, fold in the chocolate chips.

5. Pour the batter into the loaf pan, smooth the top, and bake for 50 minutes, or until a toothpick inserted in the center of the loaf comes out clean.

6. Allow to cool in the pan for 30 minutes before removing and slicing.

7. Store leftovers in the refrigerator for up to a week.

TWIST

For a decadent Sunday brunch treat, frost this bread with the Vanilla Buttercream Frosting from the Protein Cake recipe on page 220!

CALORIES: 170   FAT: 13.7g   PROTEIN: 4.8g   CARBS: 7g   FIBER: 3.9g   SUGAR ALCOHOL: 0.7g

CHEESY CHICKEN BREADSTICKS

MAKES: 2 servings   **PREP TIME:** 10 minutes   **COOK TIME:** 25 minutes

You have to get creative when trying to turn some of your favorite foods into keto staples. This unique combination of chicken and cheese makes the lowest-carb breadsticks we've ever tried.

2 (5-ounce) cans chunk chicken breast in water

¼ cup grated Parmesan cheese

1 large egg

¼ cup shredded cheddar cheese

¼ cup shredded mozzarella cheese

½ teaspoon dried oregano leaves

½ teaspoon garlic powder

½ teaspoon pink Himalayan salt

Low-carb marinara sauce, for serving

1. Preheat the oven to 350°F and line a baking sheet with parchment paper.

2. Drain the chicken and place it on the parchment-lined baking sheet. Use a fork to spread it into an even layer. Bake for 10 minutes, until dried out.

3. Put the dried-out chicken in a medium-sized bowl, then add the Parmesan and egg and mix with a fork.

4. Pour the mixture back onto the parchment paper, top with another piece of parchment, and roll out using a rolling pin into an oval, about 8 by 5 inches.

5. Bake for 5 minutes. Top the chicken mixture with the cheddar cheese, mozzarella cheese, oregano, garlic powder, and salt. Bake for an additional 10 minutes, until the cheese has melted.

6. Allow to cool slightly before cutting. Slice crosswise into 8 breadsticks. Serve with marinara sauce, if desired.

TWIST

Megha likes to top these heavenly cheese sticks with sliced red onions (her favorite vegetable) and sliced mushrooms (Matt's favorite vegetable) prior to baking! We like Rao's marinara sauce for dipping.

CALORIES: 300   FAT: 16g   PROTEIN: 37.5g   CARBS: 1.5g   FIBER: 0g

NAVAJO FRY BREAD

MAKES: 8 breads (1 per serving)   **PREP TIME:** 15 minutes   **COOK TIME:** about 50 minutes

We love learning about cuisines from different cultures and incorporating elements from them into our own cooking. This simple fried bread, which was developed in the southwestern United States by the Navajo people, is perfect for loading up with chicken breast, mozzarella cheese, chopped parsley, and Sriracha sauce!

1 cup coconut oil, for frying

½ cup coconut flour

¼ cup psyllium husk powder

½ teaspoon baking powder

¼ teaspoon pink Himalayan salt

¾ cup water

¼ cup extra-virgin olive oil

4 large eggs, room temperature

NOTE

The nutritional information can't be precisely pinpointed due to the oil used for frying. We have provided information based on the bread itself, but the fat will vary based on the amount of oil that the bread absorbs.

1. Heat the coconut oil in an 8-inch skillet over medium-high heat to between 330°F and 345°F. Use a deep-fry thermometer to read the oil temperature.

2. While the oil is heating, put the coconut flour, psyllium husk powder, baking powder, and salt in a medium-sized bowl and mix well with a fork.

3. Put the water, olive oil, and eggs in another large bowl and combine with a hand mixer. Add the dry ingredients to the wet ingredients in 2 parts, mixing after each addition. Once combined, allow the dough to rest for 5 minutes.

4. Divide the dough into 8 equal-sized pieces. Using your hands, form each piece of dough into a ball, then press it between your hands into a thin disc. The dough should be as thin as possible without breaking. If the dough is too sticky to form by hand, use extra coconut flour when shaping the flatbreads.

5. Place one flatbread in the oil. Fry for 2 to 4 minutes per side, until dark brown. Remove from the oil and set on a paper towel to drain while you fry the remaining flatbreads one at a time. Allow to cool for 2 minutes before serving.

6. Store in a zip-top plastic bag in the refrigerator for up to a week. These are best reheated in a 250°F oven for 10 minutes.

plus oil from frying

CALORIES: 140   **FAT:** 10.1g   **PROTEIN:** 4.1g   **CARBS:** 8.1g   **FIBER:** 6g

COCONUT FLOUR TORTILLAS

MAKES: 16 small tortillas (4 per serving)   **PREP TIME:** 5 minutes   **COOK TIME:** 1½ to 2 hours

Who's ready for DIY taco night? Filling these easy-to-make tortillas with all kinds of delicious ingredients is a weekly activity at our house. Be sure to double up the tortillas to hold more fillings without breaking.

8 large egg whites

½ cup plus 2 tablespoons water

⅓ cup coconut flour

¼ teaspoon baking powder

TWIST

Megha likes to add seasonings such as ground cumin, garlic powder, and chili powder to the coconut flour for extra flavor before mixing it into the batter!

NOTE

If you have two 6-inch nonstick skillets, we recommend that you use both simultaneously to cook two tortillas at a time. It will seriously cut down on the cook time for this recipe!

1. Heat a small (6-inch) nonstick skillet over low heat. In a bowl, combine the egg whites and water using a whisk.

2. In another small bowl, combine the coconut flour and baking powder with a fork. Add the dry ingredients to the egg white mixture and whisk until the mixture is uniform.

3. Spray the skillet with a light coating of coconut oil spray. Using a ¼-cup measuring cup, scoop up some of the batter and place it in the center of the skillet. Tilt the pan so that the batter covers the entire surface. Cook for 5 to 7 minutes, until the tortilla is fully cooked through. When it's ready to flip, you'll be able to lift up the edges without it breaking. Flip and cook for an additional 30 seconds.

4. Set the cooked tortilla on a plate and repeat with the rest of the batter, making a total of 16 tortillas.

5. Store leftovers in a tightly sealed container in the refrigerator for up to 2 days. Reheat in a dry skillet on the stovetop over high heat for 30 seconds on each side.

VARIATION

LARGE COCONUT FLOUR TORTILLAS. We use large coconut flour tortillas to make the quesadillas on page 140. To make large tortillas, use a 9-inch nonstick skillet, and in Step 3, use a ½-cup measuring cup to scoop up the batter. The cooking time is the same. Makes 6 large tortillas (1 per serving).

CALORIES: 74   FAT: 1.3g   PROTEIN: 7.3g   CARBS: 5.3g   FIBER: 3.3g

-Chapter 3-

CLASSIC COMFORT FOODS

CHICKEN POPPER CASSEROLE

MAKES: 6 servings   **PREP TIME:** 15 minutes   **COOK TIME:** 18 minutes

Who said jalapeño poppers are only for football Sundays? Adding some chicken and turning them into a hearty casserole is the perfect excuse to make this dish any night of the week.

1½ pounds boneless, skinless chicken thighs

Pink Himalayan salt and ground black pepper

2 medium-sized jalapeño peppers

6 ounces cream cheese (¾ cup), room temperature

¼ cup heavy whipping cream

5 slices bacon, cooked and crumbled

½ cup shredded Monterey Jack cheese (about 2 ounces)

½ cup shredded cheddar cheese (about 2 ounces), divided

1 teaspoon minced garlic

¼ teaspoon onion powder

1. Preheat the oven to 400°F.

2. Heat a large skillet over medium-high heat. While the skillet is heating, chop the chicken thighs into 1-inch pieces and lightly season with salt and pepper.

3. Spray the hot skillet with coconut oil spray, then add the chicken. Sauté on all sides until cooked through, 5 to 7 minutes.

4. Meanwhile, seed and mince one-and-a-half of the jalapeños and put in a small bowl; slice the remaining half into rings and set aside in another small bowl. (Remove the seeds from the rings if you don't care for heat.)

5. When the chicken is cooked, add the cream cheese and heavy cream and stir to combine.

6. To the chicken mixture, add the minced jalapeños and about four-fifths of the crumbled bacon; stir to combine. Add the Monterey Jack cheese and ¼ cup of the cheddar cheese and stir until melted. Add the garlic powder, onion powder, 1 teaspoon of salt, and ¼ teaspoon of pepper and stir to combine, then remove from the heat.

7. Pour the mixture into a 13 by 9-inch baking dish and spread evenly using a rubber spatula. Top with the remaining cheddar cheese and crumbled bacon and the sliced jalapeños. Bake for 10 minutes, then turn the oven to broil and broil for 2 minutes, until the cheese has melted and browned. Serve hot.

CALORIES: 372   FAT: 27.2g   PROTEIN: 30.7g   CARBS: 2.5g   FIBER: 1g

LOADED CAULIFLOWER

MAKES: 8 servings   PREP TIME: 20 minutes   COOK TIME: 5 minutes

The age-old keto dilemma: what do I have with my steak tonight? We think this loaded cauliflower is a pretty good answer.

2 heads cauliflower, cored and cut into florets

3 tablespoons unsalted butter, melted

¼ cup heavy whipping cream

¼ cup sour cream

1 teaspoon pink Himalayan salt

½ teaspoon ground black pepper

¼ cup shredded cheddar cheese

4 slices bacon, cooked and crumbled

FOR GARNISH (OPTIONAL):

Chopped fresh chives

Sour cream

1. Set a large pot of water over high heat. Add the cauliflower florets and bring to a boil. Boil for 10 to 15 minutes, until fork-tender. Drain the cauliflower.

2. Put half of the florets in a food processor and pulse for 30 seconds. Add half of the melted butter, half of the cream, and half of the sour cream and process until smooth. As you process, the mixture will work its way up the sides of the processor. When this happens, stop processing and push the mixture down using a rubber spatula.

3. Add half of the salt and pepper to the cauliflower mixture in the blender and pulse to combine. Pour the cauliflower mash into a 13 by 9-inch baking dish.

4. Repeat with the remaining cauliflower, butter, cream, sour cream, salt, and pepper, then add to the baking dish.

5. Smooth the top of the mash with a rubber spatula, then top with the shredded cheese and crumbled bacon. Broil for 2 to 4 minutes, until the cheese has melted and slightly browned. Sprinkle the top with chives and garnish each serving with a dollop of sour cream, if desired.

6. Store leftovers in a sealed container in the refrigerator for up to a week. Reheat in the microwave for 30 to 60 seconds.

CALORIES: 149   FAT: 11.4g   PROTEIN: 5.4g   CARBS: 8.4g   FIBER: 3.6g

SPICY CAULIFLOWER BITES

MAKES: 4 servings **PREP TIME:** 10 minutes **COOK TIME:** 20 minutes

If we're using the oven to prepare dinner, then chances are we're throwing in a double order of Spicy Cauliflower Bites to go along with it. Anytime you bite into a cauliflower floret and mistake it for a chicken wing, you know you've got a good recipe on your hands.

1 head cauliflower, cored and cut into florets

2 tablespoons extra-virgin olive oil

1½ teaspoons chili powder

1½ teaspoons garlic powder

1½ teaspoons paprika

1 teaspoon pink Himalayan salt

½ teaspoon baking powder

Sliced scallions, for topping (optional)

Blue cheese dressing, store-bought or homemade (see Notes), for serving (optional)

1. Preheat the oven to 450°F and line a rimmed baking sheet with parchment paper.

2. Put the cauliflower florets in a large mixing bowl. Add the remaining ingredients, except the scallions and blue cheese dressing, and, using your hands, toss to coat the cauliflower evenly. Pour the florets onto the lined baking sheet and spread into an even layer.

3. Roast for 20 minutes, or until fork-tender. Serve immediately, topped with sliced scallions and with blue cheese dressing on the side, if desired.

4. Store in a sealed container in the refrigerator for up to 3 days. Reheat in a preheated 250°F oven for 10 minutes, or until crispy.

TWIST

On Michigan game days, Matt loves to eat these alongside our Chipotle Dry-Rub Wings (page 142)!

NOTES

The addition of baking powder helps dry out the cauliflower so that you get the crispiest bites possible!

Store-bought blue cheese dressing contains soybean oil; however, we are comfortable using it sparingly as a dipping sauce for these bites (or for chicken wings, of course!) or to dress the occasional salad.

CALORIES: 105   **FAT:** 7.3g   **PROTEIN:** 3.3g   **CARBS:** 9.3g   **FIBER:** 4g

SPAGHETTI WITH MEAT SAUCE

MAKES: 1 serving   **PREP TIME:** 10 minutes   **COOK TIME:** 12 minutes

Zucchini noodles are our favorite pasta replacement. Cooked lightly, these noodles pair perfectly with any traditional pasta sauce, especially this simple and flavorful meat sauce. This recipe makes just one serving of zucchini noodles because we have found that they do not keep and reheat well. Making them fresh is a lot tastier!

SAUCE:

Makes 1⅓ cups (4 servings)

1 (14½-ounce) can whole peeled tomatoes

1 tablespoon extra-virgin olive oil

½ teaspoon garlic powder

½ teaspoon dried oregano leaves

½ teaspoon dried parsley

¼ teaspoon onion powder

¼ teaspoon red pepper flakes

⅛ teaspoon pink Himalayan salt

3 to 5 drops of liquid stevia

SPAGHETTI (FOR 1 SERVING):

1 medium-sized zucchini

4 ounces ground beef (80/20)

Grated Parmesan cheese, for topping (optional; omit for dairy-free)

1. Make the sauce: Put the tomatoes, olive oil, seasonings, and stevia in a blender and blend until the consistency is smooth. Pour the mixture into a small saucepan and cook over medium heat for 5 to 7 minutes, until reduced by about one-third. Remove from the heat.

2. Make the spaghetti: Spiral-slice the zucchini into noodles. Put in a small bowl and set aside.

3. Heat a medium-sized skillet over medium-high heat and spray with coconut oil spray. Put the ground beef in the hot skillet and cook through, stirring to break up the meat as it cooks. Add ⅓ cup of the sauce to the ground beef and stir to combine.

4. Place a second medium-sized skillet over medium-high heat. When it is hot, place the zucchini noodles and 2 to 3 tablespoons of water in the skillet. Cover with the lid and steam for 1 to 2 minutes, until just tender. Remove the lid, drain the noodles, and transfer the noodles to a bowl. Top with the meat sauce and grated Parmesan, if desired.

5. Store the remaining sauce in a sealed container in the refrigerator for up to 2 weeks.

CALORIES: 327   FAT: 21g   PROTEIN: 24g   CARBS: 11g   FIBER: 3g

CREAMY WHITE CHILI

MAKES: 6 servings **PREP TIME:** 15 minutes **COOK TIME:** 1 hour 20 minutes

Chili is a household favorite of ours. All you really have to do is throw everything into a pot and let it cook for an hour. So simple! Green chilies and jalapeño peppers give this white chili that signature Southwestern flavor.

1½ pounds boneless, skinless chicken thighs

2 tablespoons unsalted butter

2 tablespoons extra-virgin olive oil

½ medium-sized white onion, diced

3 cloves garlic, minced

1 (4-ounce) can green chilies

½ medium-sized jalapeño pepper, seeded and chopped

4 cups low-sodium chicken broth

2 teaspoons ground cumin

½ teaspoon paprika

½ teaspoon pink Himalayan salt

¼ teaspoon chili powder

¼ teaspoon ground black pepper

¼ cup heavy whipping cream

⅓ cup shredded Monterey Jack cheese

FOR GARNISH (OPTIONAL):

Sliced avocado

Sliced jalapeño peppers

Roughly chopped fresh cilantro

1. Put the chicken thighs in a large saucepan and fill with water, submerging the chicken entirely. Boil over high heat for 20 minutes, or until the chicken is fully cooked through.

2. Drain the chicken and set on a plate to cool. Once cool, shred the chicken using 2 forks or your hands. Set aside.

3. Put the butter and olive oil in a large pot over medium heat. Once the butter has melted, add the onion and garlic and cook for 3 minutes, or until the onion is translucent and fragrant.

4. Add the green chilies and jalapeño and cook for 2 minutes. Turn the heat up to medium-high, add the broth, and bring to a boil.

5. Add the shredded chicken and seasonings, stir, and cover with a lid. Turn the heat down to low and simmer for 45 minutes.

6. Add the cream and cheese and stir. Allow to cook with the lid off for an additional 10 minutes, then remove from the heat. Serve garnished with avocado, jalapeños, and cilantro, if desired.

7. Store leftovers in a sealed container in the refrigerator for up to a week or freeze for up to 2 months. Reheat in the microwave if refrigerated or on the stovetop if frozen.

TWIST

Chili is one of Megha's favorite foods. When she heats up a bowl, she likes to add shirataki noodles to give it a toothsome bite!

CALORIES: 278   FAT: 18g   PROTEIN: 24.2g   CARBS: 3.3g   FIBER: 0.5g

CHICKEN TENDERS

MAKES: 4 servings   PREP TIME: 10 minutes   COOK TIME: 33 minutes

We've tried every type of low-carb breading there is, and this combination of pork rinds and Italian herbs and spices is the one we keep going back to. It reminds Matt of the breaded chicken his grandma used to make for him growing up.

3 ounces pork rinds

2 teaspoons dried oregano leaves

2 teaspoons garlic powder

2 teaspoons onion powder

2 teaspoons red pepper flakes

1 teaspoon pink Himalayan salt

2 large eggs

2 tablespoons heavy whipping cream

1 pound chicken tenders

BBQ sauce, homemade (page 246) or store-bought, for serving (optional)

1. Preheat the oven to 350°F and line a rimmed baking sheet with parchment paper.

2. Put the pork rinds and seasonings in a food processor and pulse until crumbly and combined. Pour onto a dinner plate. Set aside.

3. Crack the eggs into a small bowl and add the cream. Combine using a whisk.

4. Pat the chicken tenders dry and, working in batches, dip them in the egg wash and then dredge them in the seasoned pork rinds. Once they are fully coated, lay them on the lined baking sheet in a single layer.

5. Bake the tenders for 30 minutes, then turn the oven to broil and broil for 2 to 3 minutes, until the chicken is cooked through and the breading is browned. Serve with BBQ sauce for dipping, if desired.

6. Store leftovers in a sealed container in the refrigerator for up to 3 days. Reheat in the oven for maximum crispiness.

CALORIES: 305   FAT: 16g   PROTEIN: 38g   CARBS: 3.3g   FIBER: 1g

CRISPY CHICKEN THIGHS WITH PAN SAUCE

MAKES: 4 servings   **PREP TIME:** 10 minutes   **COOK TIME:** 35 minutes

You'll probably notice that after you cook skin-on chicken thighs, you're left with a ton of delicious drippings in the pan. Don't let that flavor go to waste! This pan sauce takes just a couple of minutes to whip up and adds a bright flavor to the crispy chicken thighs.

4 boneless, skin-on chicken thighs (about 1 pound)

PAN SAUCE:

¼ medium-sized white onion, finely diced

4 cloves garlic, minced

½ teaspoon pink Himalayan salt

¼ teaspoon ground black pepper

¼ cup low-sodium chicken broth

¼ cup dry white wine

1 teaspoon unflavored beef gelatin powder

2 tablespoons unsalted butter

¼ cup chopped fresh parsley

Juice of ¼ lemon

TWIST

Sometimes Megha likes to change it up and use red wine to make the reduction!

1. Preheat the oven to 350°F.

2. Heat a medium-sized oven-safe skillet over medium heat. Grease the skillet with coconut oil spray, pat the chicken thighs dry, and lay them skin side down in the pan.

3. Using a spatula, press down on the thighs so that the entire surface of the skin is in contact with the hot skillet. Sear for 10 minutes, then flip the thighs over and put the skillet in the oven. Bake for 15 minutes, or until the chicken is fully cooked through.

4. Make the pan sauce: Remove the thighs from the skillet and set aside. Return the pan to the stovetop over medium heat. Add the onion and garlic and cook until the onion is translucent. Season with the salt and pepper.

5. Add the chicken broth, wine, and gelatin to the pan and scrape the bottom using a metal spatula to release and combine the pan drippings with the liquid. Simmer until the drippings are nearly fully reduced, then add the butter and stir with the spatula. Cook for 2 to 3 minutes, until the butter is incorporated into the sauce.

6. Add the parsley and lemon juice and stir to combine. Return the thighs to the pan and spoon some of the sauce over the top. Serve family-style, from the skillet, or slice the thighs crosswise and serve plated with the pan sauce over the chicken or on the side.

7. Store leftovers in a tightly sealed container in the refrigerator for up to 5 days. Reheat in the microwave for 60 to 90 seconds.

CALORIES: 308   **FAT:** 21g   **PROTEIN:** 35.5g   **CARBS:** 3.3g   **FIBER:** 0.3g

MEXICAN CHORIZO CASSEROLE

MAKES: 8 servings   **PREP TIME:** 15 minutes   **COOK TIME:** 40 minutes

We're always trying to use spicy Mexican chorizo in new recipes. The flavor is so intense and assertive that it is hard to come away with a disappointing dish. We like to make this casserole on the weekend and have it ready throughout the week in case we don't have time to cook. Failure to prepare is preparing to fail!

1 pound fresh (raw) bulk chorizo

¼ medium-sized white onion, diced

5 ounces cream cheese (½ cup plus 2 tablespoons)

¼ cup sour cream

1 small tomato, diced

1 (15-ounce) bag frozen spinach, thawed and drained

1 (4-ounce) can green chilies

¼ teaspoon pink Himalayan salt

¾ cup shredded cheddar cheese (about 3 ounces)

1. Preheat the oven to 350°F.

2. Heat a 12-inch cast-iron skillet or other oven-safe skillet over medium-high heat. Put the chorizo in the skillet and partially cook, crumbling the sausage with a spatula as it cooks. Add the onion and cook until softened, about 5 minutes.

3. Add the cream cheese, sour cream, tomato, spinach, chilies, and salt and stir to combine. When all the ingredients are evenly incorporated, remove from the heat.

4. Flatten out the surface of the casserole and sprinkle on the cheese, covering the entire surface.

5. Bake for 30 minutes, until the cheese is melted and slightly browned on top. Allow to rest for 5 minutes, then cut into 8 wedges and serve.

6. Store leftovers in a sealed container in the refrigerator for up to 10 days or freeze for up to a month. Reheat in the microwave for 60 to 90 seconds.

CALORIES: 379   FAT: 32.1g   PROTEIN: 17g   CARBS: 5.5g   FIBER: 0.6g

BACON AND CRAB MAC AND CHEESE

MAKES: 4 servings   PREP TIME: 10 minutes   COOK TIME: 30 minutes

We met in the amazing city of San Francisco, and on one of our first dates, we bought crab mac and cheese from a vendor on Fisherman's Wharf. It was the moment we first bonded over our shared love of food, so it was only right that we re-created that experience for our first cookbook.

3 slices bacon, chopped

¼ medium-sized white onion, diced

1 head cauliflower, cored and cut into florets

2 teaspoons garlic powder

½ teaspoon pink Himalayan salt

1 (6-ounce) can lump crabmeat

2 tablespoons unsalted butter

¼ cup heavy whipping cream

1 cup shredded white cheddar cheese (about 4 ounces)

½ teaspoon dried parsley leaves, plus extra for garnish (optional)

¼ teaspoon ground black pepper

2 crab legs, for garnish (optional)

1. Preheat the oven to 425°F.

2. Heat a large skillet over medium-high heat. Put the chopped bacon in the skillet and cook three-quarters of the way through, about 3 minutes. Add the onion and cook for 1 to 2 minutes, until tender.

3. Add the cauliflower florets, garlic powder, and salt and stir to combine. Place a lid over the skillet and steam the cauliflower for 5 to 7 minutes, until cooked through. Remove the lid and continue to cook for an additional 5 minutes.

4. Remove the skillet from the heat and add the crabmeat. Toss gently with the cauliflower, then set aside.

5. Put the butter and cream in a small saucepan over low heat. Allow the butter to melt, stirring often.

6. When the butter is completely melted, add the cheese, parsley, and pepper and stir to combine. When the cheese is melted, pour the cheese mixture over the cauliflower and crabmeat and toss, coating the cauliflower and crabmeat evenly. Pour the mac and cheese into an 8-inch square baking dish and bake for 10 minutes, until slightly browned on top.

7. If desired, while the mac and cheese is baking, steam a couple of crab legs until they turn bright pink. Serve the mac and cheese garnished with the crab legs, along with some more parsley.

8. Store leftovers in a sealed container in the refrigerator for up to a week. Reheat in the microwave for 60 to 90 seconds, until the cheese is melted.

CALORIES: 320   FAT: 23g   PROTEIN: 20.8g   CARBS: 10.5g   FIBER: 4g

CHICKEN NOODLE-LESS SOUP

MAKES: 6 servings   PREP TIME: 15 minutes   COOK TIME: 30 minutes

This is the chicken noodle soup that your mom used to make, but without the noodles. There's nothing quite like enjoying a bowl of this soup while snuggled up with your pets watching a rerun of *It's Always Sunny in Philadelphia* on a Sunday morning.

1½ pounds boneless, skinless chicken breasts

1½ teaspoons pink Himalayan salt, divided

½ teaspoon ground black pepper, divided

1½ tablespoons ghee or coconut oil

3 tablespoons unsalted butter

3 stalks celery, chopped

½ medium-sized white onion, diced

1 teaspoon minced garlic

6 ounces baby bella mushrooms, sliced

1 teaspoon dried oregano leaves

½ teaspoon poultry seasoning

5 cups low-sodium chicken broth

2 teaspoons minced fresh parsley, plus extra for garnish (optional)

1. Cut the chicken into bite-sized pieces and season with ½ teaspoon of the salt and ¼ teaspoon of the pepper. Heat a large pot over medium-high heat. Place the ghee in the hot pot, then add the chicken. Sauté until cooked through, 5 to 7 minutes. Remove the chicken from the pot and set aside.

2. Turn the heat down to medium and melt the butter in the pot. Add the celery and onion and allow to cook down for 2 to 3 minutes, stirring frequently. Add the garlic and mushrooms, stir to combine, and cook for an additional 1 minute.

3. Return the cooked chicken to the pot. Add the remaining teaspoon of salt, remaining ¼ teaspoon of pepper, oregano, and poultry seasoning and stir to combine. Turn the heat back up to medium-high, pour in the chicken broth, stir, and bring to a boil. Once boiling, cover the pot with a lid, reduce the heat to medium-low, and simmer for 15 minutes.

4. Before serving, stir in the parsley. Garnish each bowl with additional parsley, if desired.

TIP

Change up the vegetables in this soup to make it better suited for your or your family's taste buds!

CALORIES: 218   FAT: 12.2g   PROTEIN: 24.5g   CARBS: 3.7g   FIBER: 1g

CREAMY CHICKEN ALFREDO

MAKES: 1 serving   **PREP TIME:** 5 minutes   **COOK TIME:** 20 minutes

If you've never tried shirataki noodles, you're missing out! They are nearly zero-calorie noodles made from konjac fiber. If you take the necessary steps of rinsing and drying the noodles, they make a delicious base for this creamy Alfredo sauce. Alfredo sauce deserves the best-quality Romano or Parmesan cheese you can find!

1 (4-ounce) boneless, skinless chicken thigh

Pink Himalayan salt and ground black pepper

1 (8-ounce) package shirataki noodles

SAUCE:

2 tablespoons unsalted butter

¼ cup heavy whipping cream

¼ cup grated pecorino Romano or Parmigiano-Reggiano cheese, plus extra for garnish (optional)

1 teaspoon dried parsley leaves, plus extra for garnish (optional)

¼ teaspoon garlic powder

¼ teaspoon pink Himalayan salt

⅛ teaspoon ground black pepper

FOR SERVING (OPTIONAL):

1 Low-Carb Dinner Roll (page 82) (omit for egg-free)

1. Cook the chicken: Heat a medium-sized skillet over medium-high heat and grease with coconut oil spray. Pat the chicken dry and season with salt and pepper. Put the chicken in the hot skillet and cook for about 3 minutes on each side, until the internal temperature reaches 165°F. Remove from the skillet and slice into strips; set aside.

2. Prepare the noodles: Turn the heat under the skillet down to low. Rinse the noodles with hot water and drain. Pat them as dry as possible using paper towels and add to the hot skillet. Stir them around using tongs or a spatula for about 5 minutes, until they have dried out slightly. Turn off the heat, leaving the noodles in the skillet.

3. Make the sauce: Put the butter and cream in a small saucepan over low heat. Allow the butter to melt, stirring often. Once the butter is melted, add the rest of the sauce ingredients. Cook, stirring continuously using a rubber spatula, until the cheese is melted and the sauce is thick.

4. Pour the sauce over the noodles in the skillet and turn the heat to medium to reheat the noodles. Add the chicken and, using the tongs, toss to coat the noodles and chicken thoroughly with the sauce.

5. Serve garnished with additional dried parsley and grated Romano cheese, and with a low-carb dinner roll on the side, if desired.

CALORIES: 646   FAT: 54g   PROTEIN: 33g   CARBS: 8g   FIBER: 3g

SOUTHERN BAKED CHICKEN

MAKES: 6 servings **PREP TIME:** 15 minutes **COOK TIME:** 40 minutes

All the flavor of fried chicken with none of the cleanup! We've found that ground-up pork rinds make the most flavorful breading for low-carb cooking, and with the right mix of seasonings, they can be used as breadcrumbs for any type of cooking.

4 ounces pork rinds

½ teaspoon dried thyme leaves

½ teaspoon paprika

½ teaspoon pink Himalayan salt

¼ teaspoon garlic powder

¼ teaspoon cayenne pepper

¼ teaspoon ground black pepper

3 pounds bone-in, skin-on chicken thighs and legs

1. Preheat the oven to 400°F and place a wire baking rack inside a rimmed baking sheet.

2. Place the pork rinds and seasonings in a food processor and process until finely ground. Put the mixture into a gallon-sized zip-top plastic bag.

3. Pat the chicken dry. In batches, put it in the bag with the seasoned pork rinds and shake until all the chicken is thoroughly coated. Place the coated chicken on the baking rack.

4. Bake for 40 minutes, or until the chicken is cooked through.

TIP

If you like your chicken extra-crispy like we do, broil the chicken for 2 minutes after baking to create a crispier skin!

CALORIES: 469   FAT: 26.7g   PROTEIN: 54.8g   CARBS: 0.5g   FIBER: 0g

MAMA'S MEATLOAF

MAKES: 8 servings   **PREP TIME:** 15 minutes   **COOK TIME:** 53 minutes

When we make meatloaf, we like to use hemp hearts instead of breadcrumbs to add nutrients and healthy fats. The hemp hearts give this dish a signature flavor that will have your dinner guests trying to guess the secret ingredient.

2 tablespoons extra-virgin olive oil

½ small white onion, diced

5 cloves garlic, minced

2 teaspoons dried thyme leaves

½ teaspoon pink Himalayan salt

½ teaspoon ground black pepper

2 pounds ground beef (80/20)

¼ cup hemp hearts

2 teaspoons soy sauce

TOPPING:

6 tablespoons reduced-sugar ketchup

2 tablespoons apple cider vinegar

1 tablespoon Frank's RedHot sauce

¼ teaspoon liquid stevia

1. Preheat the oven to 350°F and line a rimmed baking sheet with parchment paper.

2. Heat a medium-sized skillet over medium heat. Put the olive oil in the hot skillet, then add the onion and garlic. Cook for 2 to 3 minutes, until the onion is translucent. Add the thyme, salt, and pepper and stir to combine. Transfer the onion mixture to a large bowl and allow to cool.

3. When the onion mixture is cool, add the ground beef, hemp hearts, and soy sauce to the bowl. Using your hands, mix the ingredients together until well combined, then form the mixture into a loaf shape in an 8 by 4-inch loaf pan.

4. Flip the loaf pan over onto the lined baking sheet and gently remove the loaf pan. Bake the meatloaf for 20 minutes.

5. While the meatloaf is baking, make the topping: In a small bowl, whisk together the ketchup, vinegar, hot sauce, and stevia.

6. After 20 minutes, remove the meatloaf from the oven. Cover the surface with the topping and bake for 30 more minutes, until the meatloaf is cooked through and has reached an internal temperature of at least 155°F. Let cool on the pan for a bit, then cut into 8 equal-sized slices and serve.

TIP

If you double the topping recipe, you can apply another coat of the topping before serving the meatloaf!

CALORIES: 351   FAT: 27.5g   PROTEIN: 21g   CARBS: 3.1g   FIBER: 1g

SPICY TUNA HAND ROLLS

MAKES: 6 servings   **PREP TIME:** 10 minutes

We're both certified sushi addicts. We had a fun tradition when we lived in San Francisco: on Saturday nights when we didn't want to go out with our friends, we would go to the sushi restaurant around the block in sweatpants and order a bunch of sushi rolls and talk about life. These hand rolls are great because you get that sushi flavor you've been missing, but without the rice.

TUNA:

12 ounces sushi-grade ahi tuna, finely chopped (see Note)

2 tablespoons Sriracha sauce

1 tablespoon mayonnaise, homemade (page 248) or store-bought

1 teaspoon toasted sesame oil

HAND ROLLS:

3 sheets nori

1 medium-sized avocado, thinly sliced

½ cucumber, julienned

Black and white sesame seeds, for garnish (optional)

Soy sauce, for serving

1. Put the tuna, Sriracha, mayonnaise, and sesame oil in a small bowl and mix with a spoon.

2. Cut the nori sheets in half lengthwise to create 6 rectangular wrappers.

3. Place a wrapper on the palm of one of your hands. Put 2 ounces of tuna and 3 or 4 slices each of avocado and cucumber on the left end of the wrapper, on a diagonal to make rolling easier. Starting from the bottom-left corner, tightly roll into a cone shape, moistening the edge of the nori to create a seal. Garnish the top of the roll with sesame seeds, if desired. Repeat with the remaining ingredients.

4. Serve the rolls with soy sauce. These are best eaten immediately, as they don't store well.

NOTE

When purchasing tuna to use in these hand rolls, look for frozen wild-caught tuna to ensure that the bacteria is killed off in the freezing process. Buying fresh tuna can be risky when you are planning to consume it raw.

CALORIES: 133   FAT: 6.3g   PROTEIN: 15.2g   CARBS: 4.2g   FIBER: 2.3g

DOUBLE BACON CHEESEBURGER

MAKES: 1 serving   **PREP TIME:** 5 minutes   **COOK TIME:** 20 minutes

This American classic happens to be the perfect keto meal once you find a good replacement for the bun. We've tried a bunch of different options, but the sturdiness of collard greens makes them our favorite choice.

4 slices bacon

8 ounces ground beef (80/20)

½ teaspoon garlic powder

½ teaspoon onion powder

½ teaspoon pink Himalayan salt

½ teaspoon ground black pepper

2 slices cheddar cheese

4 collard green leaves

1. Heat a cast-iron skillet over medium heat. Put the bacon slices in the pan and cook for 4 minutes on each side, or until crispy. Remove and set on a paper towel; leave the bacon drippings in the pan.

2. Form the ground beef into two patties, about ½ inch thick. Season the patties on both sides with the garlic powder, onion powder, salt, and pepper. Increase the heat to medium-high and place the patties in the skillet. Sear the burgers for 4 to 6 minutes, then flip and top each with a slice of cheddar cheese and 2 slices of bacon. Cook for another 4 to 6 minutes, until the desired doneness is achieved. (Note: For medium-done burgers, cook for 4 minutes on each side; for medium-well, 5 minutes on each side; and well-done, 6 minutes on each side.) Remove the patties from the skillet and allow to rest for 5 minutes before assembling.

3. Using a paring knife, remove the center stem from each collard leaf. Lay the leaves on top of one another with half of each leaf overlapping.

4. Stack the beef patties on top of one another in the center of the collard greens. Fold the edges in to completely enclose the patties. Use a toothpick to hold everything together, if desired.

TWIST

Matt always adds a fried egg to his burgers, whether we make them at home or get them out!

CALORIES: 820   FAT: 60g   PROTEIN: 65g   CARBS: 6g   FIBER: 1g

SAAG PANEER

MAKES: 4 servings   **PREP TIME:** 10 minutes   **COOK TIME:** 20 minutes

Matt had never tried Indian food until he met Megha, but he quickly fell in love. Saag paneer was the first Indian dish he tried, and to this day it's still his favorite. If you've never had paneer, you're missing out! It's a frying cheese that you can find at any Indian grocer. It is often used as the main protein in vegetarian dishes.

2 tablespoons ghee, divided

8 ounces paneer, cubed

1/3 medium-sized white onion, roughly chopped

3 cloves garlic, minced

1 (1/2-inch) piece fresh ginger, grated

1 small tomato, diced

4 cups frozen spinach, thawed

2 1/2 teaspoons garam masala

1 1/2 teaspoons turmeric powder

1 teaspoon chili powder

1 teaspoon pink Himalayan salt

1/2 cup heavy whipping cream

1. Heat 1 tablespoon of the ghee in a large skillet over medium-high heat. Add the paneer and cook until browned and crispy, 5 to 7 minutes, tossing every couple of minutes. Remove from the pan and set aside.

2. Turn the heat down to medium and add the remaining tablespoon of ghee to the hot pan. Add the onion, garlic, and ginger and stir to combine. Cook until the onion is translucent.

3. Add the tomato and spinach and stir thoroughly. Cook for 3 to 5 minutes, until most of the water from the tomatoes and spinach has evaporated.

4. Add the seasonings and cream and stir to combine. Cook for 5 minutes, until the sauce has thickened. Return the paneer to the pan to reheat for a few minutes. Serve immediately.

5. Store leftovers in a sealed container in the refrigerator for up to 4 days.

TWIST

Megha prefers to eat her saag paneer with Low-Carb Flatbread (from the gyro recipe on page 148), while Matt likes cauliflower rice.

CALORIES: 386   **FAT:** 31g   **PROTEIN:** 15.3g   **CARBS:** 8.3g   **FIBER:** 1g

THAI YELLOW CHICKEN CURRY

MAKES: 2 servings   PREP TIME: 10 minutes   COOK TIME: 20 minutes

Everyone needs a little Thai curry in their life. Whenever we get into a dinner rut, we turn to this yellow curry to break up the monotony.

2 tablespoons coconut oil, divided

12 ounces boneless, skinless chicken thighs, cubed

1 tablespoon minced garlic

1 tablespoon grated fresh ginger

½ medium-sized white onion, roughly chopped

2 tablespoons low-sodium chicken broth

1 tablespoon soy sauce

1 tablespoon curry powder

1 teaspoon red pepper flakes

¼ teaspoon pink Himalayan salt

7 ounces (½ can) coconut milk

1½ cups fresh broccoli florets

1 tablespoon minced fresh cilantro

1. Heat 1 tablespoon of the coconut oil in a large skillet over medium-high heat. Add the cubed chicken and cook through, 5 to 7 minutes. Remove from the pan and set aside.

2. Turn the heat down to medium and add the remaining tablespoon of coconut oil to the skillet. Add the garlic, ginger, and onion and stir. Cook until the mixture is fragrant and the onion is slightly translucent, 2 to 3 minutes.

3. Add the broth, soy sauce, curry powder, red pepper flakes, and salt and stir. When everything is thoroughly combined, add the coconut milk and cook, stirring often, until fully incorporated and heated through, 3 to 5 minutes.

4. Return the chicken to the pan and add the broccoli. Stir so that everything is coated. Cook for an additional 3 to 5 minutes, until the broccoli is tender and the chicken is heated through. Stir in the cilantro and serve immediately.

5. Store leftovers in a sealed container in the refrigerator for up to 4 days.

CALORIES: 517   FAT: 36g   PROTEIN: 34g   CARBS: 16g   FIBER: 4.5g

BUFFALO CHICKEN CRUST PIZZA

MAKES: 2 servings **PREP TIME:** 10 minutes **COOK TIME:** 30 minutes

As soon as we figured out the recipe for Cheesy Chicken Breadsticks (page 88), we knew we had to take that same dough and use it make a Buffalo chicken pizza. You'll never buy bottled Buffalo sauce again once you see how easy it is to make from scratch!

BUFFALO SAUCE:

¼ cup Frank's RedHot sauce

¼ cup (½ stick) unsalted butter

2¼ teaspoons apple cider vinegar

CRUST:

2 (5-ounce) cans chunk chicken breast in water, drained

¼ cup grated Parmesan cheese

1 large egg

TOPPINGS:

4 ounces fresh mozzarella cheese, sliced

1 tablespoon sliced scallions (optional)

TWIST

Megha likes to dip her slices in blue cheese dressing to up the fat-to-protein ratio and maximize the flavor!

1. Preheat the oven to 350°F and line a pizza stone or metal pizza pan with parchment paper.

2. Make the sauce: Put the hot sauce, butter, and vinegar in a small saucepan over medium heat. Once the butter melts, stir to combine and remove from the heat. Set aside.

3. Prepare the crust: Spread the drained chicken on the lined pizza stone/pan and bake for 10 minutes to remove all the moisture. Remove from the oven and transfer the chicken to a medium-sized bowl. Increase the oven temperature to 500°F.

4. To the bowl with the chicken, add the Parmesan cheese and egg. Mix thoroughly with a fork.

5. Place a clean sheet of parchment paper on the counter and pour the chicken mixture onto it. Spread the chicken into a thin layer with a rubber spatula. Place another piece of parchment paper on top of the chicken mixture and flatten it into a ¼-inch-thick circle using a rolling pin. Remove the top piece of parchment, transfer the bottom piece of parchment with the crust on it to the pizza stone/pan, and bake the crust for 8 minutes, until slightly browned and hardened.

6. Remove the crust from the oven and top with the Buffalo sauce and mozzarella cheese. Bake for 6 to 8 more minutes, until the cheese is melted and starting to brown. Remove from the oven, top with the sliced scallions, if using, and cut into 6 slices.

7. Store leftovers in a sealed container in the refrigerator for up to 3 days. Reheat in a 250°F oven.

CALORIES: 600   FAT: 44.5g   PROTEIN: 47.5g   CARBS: 1.5g   FIBER: 0g

SPICY SHRIMP FRIED RICE

MAKES: 4 servings   **PREP TIME:** 15 minutes   **COOK TIME:** 15 minutes

If there is one dish that summarizes the last year of our lives, it is shrimp fried rice. It's quick, it's easy, you can make it all in one pot, and it never disappoints. We love the crispy fried rice and the fresh Asian flavors.

¼ teaspoon cayenne pepper

¼ teaspoon chili powder

¼ teaspoon paprika

¼ teaspoon pink Himalayan salt

¼ teaspoon ground black pepper

1 pound medium-sized shrimp, peeled and deveined

2 tablespoons ghee, divided

4 cups riced cauliflower (see Tip)

½ medium-sized white onion, finely chopped

2 teaspoons minced fresh ginger

1 cup fresh broccoli florets, chopped

3 tablespoons soy sauce

1 tablespoon Sriracha sauce

1½ teaspoons unseasoned rice wine vinegar

2 large eggs

2 teaspoons toasted sesame oil

FOR GARNISH (OPTIONAL):

Sliced scallions

Black and white sesame seeds

1. Put the cayenne, chili powder, paprika, salt, and pepper in a medium-sized bowl. Mix to blend, then add the shrimp. Toss the shrimp in the seasoning blend until evenly coated.

2. Heat 1 tablespoon of the ghee in a large skillet over medium-high heat. Place the seasoned shrimp in the hot skillet and cook until pink, about 2 minutes on each side. Remove to a small bowl and set aside.

3. Add the remaining tablespoon of ghee to the hot skillet and pour in the riced cauliflower. Spread it out with a spatula so it lies flat on the surface of the skillet and cook until it crisps up, 3 to 5 minutes.

4. Stir the rice, then add the onion and ginger. Cook for 2 minutes, until the onion is slightly tender. Add the broccoli and cook for 1 to 2 minutes, until bright green in color. Add the soy sauce, Sriracha, and vinegar. Combine using the spatula.

5. Make a well in the center of the skillet and crack in the eggs. Scramble using the spatula, then combine with the rest of the contents of the skillet.

6. Add the shrimp and toss to combine. Drizzle with the sesame oil and garnish with sliced scallions and sesame seeds, if desired. Serve immediately.

7. Store leftovers in a sealed container in the refrigerator for up to 4 days. Reheat in the microwave for 60 to 90 seconds.

TIP

If you don't have pre-riced cauliflower on hand, simply chop the florets from a large head of cauliflower into chunks and pulse in a food processor until the cauliflower is in rice-sized pieces, about 30 seconds.

CALORIES: 283   FAT: 13.3g   PROTEIN: 31.8g   CARBS: 12.8g   FIBER: 4g

CHOCOLATE ALMOND BUTTER SHAKE

MAKES: 1 serving   PREP TIME: 3 minutes

Shakes used to be one our favorite things to order out—especially at diners! Now we love making our own shakes at home. Filled with nutrition and great taste, this shake serves double duty as a great post-workout fuel source and a dessert, especially when topped with whipped cream and ground cinnamon (Matt's favorite version).

1 cup unsweetened almond milk, well chilled

2 tablespoons cocoa powder

2 tablespoons natural almond butter

1 tablespoon chia seeds

1 tablespoon unflavored protein powder

¼ teaspoon plus 5 drops of liquid stevia

¼ teaspoon pink Himalayan salt

Put all the ingredients in a blender and blend until smooth, 30 to 45 seconds. Pour into a 16-ounce glass. Enjoy cold!

TWIST

Sometimes Matt likes to moisten the rim of the serving glass in water, then dust the rim with cocoa powder to give this shake a more elegant, dessertlike feel.

CALORIES: 333   FAT: 23g   PROTEIN: 19g   CARBS: 20g   FIBER: 13g

THIN-CRUST SKILLET PIZZA

MAKES: 2 servings **PREP TIME:** 5 minutes **COOK TIME:** 5 minutes

We've come home after having a few drinks and thrown together this skillet pizza more than a few times. The crispy pan-fried cheese will make you forget all about the delivery place down the street!

1½ cups shredded mozzarella cheese

9 slices pepperoni

1 tablespoon sliced black olives

4 fresh basil leaves

1. Heat a 10-inch skillet over medium heat. Spread the shredded cheese evenly over the surface of the skillet. Cook until the cheese is almost fully melted, then layer on the pepperoni slices and olives. Continue to cook until a crust starts to form. The cheese will harden, turn brown on the bottom, and naturally lift off the skillet.

2. Once the crust has formed, turn off the heat, slide the pizza onto a plate, and garnish with basil leaves. Slice into 4 pieces and serve immediately.

CALORIES: 302   FAT: 23.5g   PROTEIN: 24g   CARBS: 4.5g   FIBER: 1g

STEAK QUESADILLAS

MAKES: 2 servings **PREP TIME:** 10 minutes (not including time to make tortillas)
COOK TIME: 30 minutes

Megha is a recovering Taco Bell addict, so this recipe is an essential at our house! Whenever we have steak for dinner, we always use the leftovers to make these quesadillas for lunch the next day.

½ pound flank steak or flat-iron steak

2 tablespoons avocado oil

1 teaspoon chili powder

½ teaspoon ground cumin

½ teaspoon garlic powder

½ teaspoon onion powder

½ teaspoon paprika

½ teaspoon pink Himalayan salt

2 Large Coconut Flour Tortillas (page 92)

⅔ cup shredded cheddar cheese

Lime wedges, for serving

Fresh cilantro, for garnish (optional)

NOTE

If using leftover steak, skip Steps 1 through 3 and omit the seasonings from the recipe. Slice the steak into strips and microwave for 30 to 60 seconds before layering it in the tortillas.

1. Make the steak: Preheat the oven to 350°F and line a rimmed baking sheet with parchment paper.

2. Combine the avocado oil, chili powder, cumin, garlic powder, onion powder, paprika, and salt in a small bowl using a spoon. Sprinkle the mixture evenly over both sides of the steak and rub it in using your hands.

3. Put the seasoned steak on the lined baking sheet and bake for 12 minutes, then turn the oven to broil and broil the steak for 2 to 3 minutes, until medium-done. Remove from the oven, transfer to a cutting board, and allow to rest for 10 minutes. Slice crosswise into ½-inch strips.

4. Make the quesadillas: Heat a 9-inch or larger skillet over medium heat and grease with coconut oil spray.

5. Place a tortilla in the skillet. Layer half the tortilla with ⅓ cup of the shredded cheese and half of the steak strips. Close the tortilla and cook on both sides until the cheese has melted and the tortilla is slightly browned. Repeat with the remaining tortilla, cheese, and steak.

6. Slice each quesadilla into 3 wedges and serve immediately with lime wedges. Garnish with cilantro, if desired.

7. Store leftover wedges in a zip-top plastic bag with the excess air removed in the refrigerator for up to 3 days.

CALORIES: 532 FAT: 36.8g PROTEIN: 41.3g CARBS: 6.3g FIBER: 4g

CHIPOTLE DRY-RUB WINGS

MAKES: 4 servings **PREP TIME:** 10 minutes **COOK TIME:** 45 minutes

Not only are chicken wings nature's perfect food, but they also happen to be a great part of a keto diet. The secret to getting a crispy wing in the oven is baking powder! Give this recipe a try, and it will be the only way you make wings in the future.

CHIPOTLE RUB:

1 tablespoon ground chipotle pepper

1 teaspoon paprika

1 teaspoon ground cumin

1 teaspoon ground mustard

1 teaspoon garlic powder

1 teaspoon onion powder

1 teaspoon pink Himalayan salt

2 pounds chicken wings

1 teaspoon baking powder

1. Preheat the oven to 250°F and place a wire baking rack inside a rimmed baking sheet.

2. Put the seasonings for the rub in a small bowl and stir with a fork. Divide the spice rub into 2 equal portions.

3. Cut the wings in half, if whole (see Tip), and place in a large zip-top plastic bag. Add the baking powder and half of the spice rub to the bag and shake thoroughly to coat the wings.

4. Lay the wings on the baking rack in a single layer. Bake for 25 minutes.

5. Turn the heat up to 450°F and bake the wings for an additional 20 minutes, until golden brown and crispy.

6. Once the wings are done, place them in a large plastic container with the remaining half of the spice rub and shake to coat. Serve immediately.

TIP

We get our wings whole, so the drumette and flat (aka wingette) with the wing tip are attached. Before we coat them, we like to cut the drumette apart from the flat and then cut the tip off the flat and discard it.

CALORIES: 507   FAT: 36g   PROTEIN: 42.3g   CARBS: 3g   FIBER: 0.3g

BEEF SATAY SKEWERS

MAKES: 4 servings   **ACTIVE PREP TIME:** 15 minutes   **INACTIVE PREP TIME:** 2 to 6 hours
COOK TIME: 10 minutes

We love exploring cuisines from around the world, and this Indonesian classic really grabbed our attention. It was a unique flavor that we'd never had before, and we must have made it for two weeks straight. We prefer these skewers grilled, but they're also great cooked on the stovetop. Either way, we can't get enough!

1 pound top sirloin

1 tablespoon fish sauce

1 teaspoon lemongrass paste

2 cloves garlic, minced

1 tablespoon avocado oil

1 tablespoon soy sauce

15 drops of liquid stevia

1 tablespoon ground coriander

½ teaspoon onion powder

½ teaspoon turmeric powder

⅛ teaspoon cayenne pepper

¼ cup water

Sliced green onions, for garnish

Peanut Sauce (page 244), for serving (optional)

Special equipment:

10 (12-inch) bamboo skewers

1. Marinate the meat: Slice the meat into ½-inch-thick slices and place in a gallon-sized zip-top plastic bag. Add the rest of the ingredients to the bag with the meat and seal, removing any excess air. Shake the bag to distribute the seasonings. Place in the refrigerator to marinate for at least 2 hours or up to 6 hours.

2. Remove the meat from the bag and skewer the slices in zigzag form; discard any remaining marinade.

3. To grill the skewers, grease the grill with coconut oil spray and preheat to high heat. To cook the skewers on the stovetop, heat a skillet over medium-high heat and grease with coconut oil spray.

4. Working in batches, cook the skewers on the preheated grill or skillet, flipping them every couple of minutes to ensure that they cook evenly. They should be fully cooked in about 8 minutes on the grill or 10 minutes on the stovetop.

5. Garnish the skewers with sliced green onions and serve warm with peanut sauce, if desired.

6. Store leftovers in a zip-top plastic bag in the refrigerator for up to 4 days.

NOTE

We feel most comfortable buying the Gourmet Garden brand of lemongrass paste and the Thai Kitchen brand of fish sauce.

CALORIES: 253   **FAT:** 15.8g   **PROTEIN:** 23.8g   **CARBS:** 4g   **FIBER:** 0.5g

CHEESE SHELL MINI TACOS

MAKES: 2 servings **PREP TIME:** 25 minutes **COOK TIME:** 25 minutes

This recipe was inspired by a trip to Chelsea Market in New York. We went to the top-rated taco stand in the city, and taco shells made out of cheese were on the menu! Can you say Taco Tuesday?

2 cups shredded cheddar cheese

8 ounces ground beef (80/20)

1 teaspoon chili powder

½ teaspoon ground cumin

½ teaspoon garlic powder

½ teaspoon pink Himalayan salt

¼ teaspoon dried oregano leaves

2 Roma tomatoes, diced

2 avocados, diced

FOR GARNISH (OPTIONAL):

Fresh cilantro leaves

Sour cream

Lime wedges

1. Preheat the oven to 350°F and line 2 rimmed baking sheets with parchment paper.

2. Make 8 (1-ounce) piles of shredded cheese, 4 per baking sheet, and flatten them slightly into 3-inch circles (they will spread).

3. Place one of the baking sheets in the oven and bake for 5 to 7 minutes, until the cheese is melted and the edges are starting to brown.

4. Meanwhile, set up a cheese shell drying station: Balance 2 long wooden spoons (about ½ inch in diameter) or similar utensils on 2 cups or bowls. You will lay the warm cheese circles over the spoon handles to make shells.

5. Remove the cheese circles from the oven and allow to cool for 1 minute before flipping them over onto the spoon handles, 2 per handle. Let the cheese cool completely before removing from the spoons and using as taco shells. Repeat with the second baking sheet of cheese circles to make a total of 8 shells.

6. While the cheese shells harden, heat a medium-sized skillet over medium-high heat and spray with coconut oil spray. Put the ground beef in the hot skillet and cook, stirring to break up the meat. When the beef is mostly cooked through, add the chili powder, cumin, garlic powder, salt, and oregano and combine with a spoon. Cook for another 5 to 7 minutes, until browned.

7. To assemble the tacos, divide the meat, diced tomatoes, and diced avocado evenly among the cheese shells. Top with cilantro, sour cream, and a squeeze of fresh lime juice, if desired.

CALORIES: 895 **FAT:** 71g **PROTEIN:** 51g **CARBS:** 14.5g **FIBER:** 11g

PHILLY FOOD CART GYROS

MAKES: **6 servings**   PREP TIME: **20 minutes**   COOK TIME: **1 hour 20 minutes**

Philadelphia was the birthplace of our food blog. During our year there, we tried all the foods the city is known for, but we kept going back to the little cart just up the road from our apartment for authentic gyros.

GYRO MEAT:

1 pound ground lamb

1 pound ground beef (80/20)

½ medium-sized white onion, diced

4 cloves garlic, minced

1 tablespoon dried oregano leaves

2 teaspoons ground cumin

½ teaspoon pink Himalayan salt

½ teaspoon ground black pepper

LOW-CARB FLATBREAD:

½ cup coconut flour

1½ tablespoons psyllium husk powder

¼ teaspoon baking powder

2 tablespoons coconut oil, melted

1 to 1½ cups hot water

FILLINGS:

½ medium-sized cucumber, thinly sliced

¼ red onion, thinly sliced

1 small tomato, thinly sliced

Fresh dill sprigs, for garnish (optional)

1. Preheat the oven to 325°F and line an 8 by 4-inch loaf pan with parchment paper for easy removal of the meat.

2. In a large bowl, use your hands to combine the lamb, beef, white onion, garlic, oregano, cumin, salt, and pepper. Once fully incorporated, form into a loaf in the lined loaf pan.

3. Bake for 1 hour, or until the internal temperature reaches at least 160°F. Remove from the oven and allow to rest in the pan while you make the flatbreads.

4. Make the flatbread: In a medium-sized bowl, combine the coconut flour, psyllium husk powder, and baking powder using a fork. Add the coconut oil and stir to combine with a wooden spoon.

5. Add the hot water and combine using the spoon, then allow to cool. Once cool, use your hands to knead the mixture into a firm dough. Allow to rest for 5 minutes.

6. Divide the dough into 6 equal portions. Working with one portion at a time, use your hands to form the dough into a ball, then place it on a piece of parchment paper. Place another piece of parchment on top and roll out to ¼-inch thickness with a rolling pin.

7. Heat a medium-sized nonstick skillet over medium-high heat. Once hot, place a flatbread in the skillet and cook for 2 to 3 minutes. You will know it is ready to flip when it starts to puff up. Flip and cook for an additional 30 to 45 seconds. Transfer to a plate. Repeat with the rest of the flatbread dough.

8. Remove the gyro meat from the loaf pan and cut it into ¼-inch-thick slices.

CALORIES: **351**   FAT: **30.3g**   PROTEIN: **20.3g**   CARBS: **10.3g**   FIBER: **5.5g**

9. To assemble the gyros, top each flatbread with 5 slices of meat and one-sixth of the cucumber, red onion, and tomato slices. Garnish with fresh dill, if desired.

10. Store leftover gyro meat and flatbread in separate zip-top plastic bags in the refrigerator for up to 4 days. Reheat the meat in the microwave for 60 to 90 seconds and the flatbread in a preheated skillet over medium heat for 1 to 2 minutes.

STICKY SESAME CHICKEN

MAKES: 2 servings PREP TIME: 10 minutes COOK TIME: 30 minutes

If you've been missing Chinese takeout, look no further than this recipe. You don't even have to leave the house! Coconut flour gives the chicken a tender breading for the thick and sticky sauce to grab hold of.

CHICKEN:

½ cup coconut oil, for the pan

½ pound boneless, skinless chicken thighs

½ teaspoon pink Himalayan salt

¼ teaspoon ground black pepper

⅓ cup coconut flour

SAUCE:

1½ teaspoons toasted sesame oil

1 clove garlic, minced

1 (½-inch) piece fresh ginger, grated

¼ cup soy sauce

2½ tablespoons unseasoned rice wine vinegar

2½ tablespoons powdered erythritol

2 tablespoons water

½ teaspoon red pepper flakes

¼ teaspoon xanthan gum

2 cups riced cauliflower (see Tip, opposite)

FOR GARNISH (OPTIONAL):

White and/or black sesame seeds

Sliced scallions

1. Heat the coconut oil in a medium-sized saucepan over medium-high heat until it reaches 330°F to 350°F on a deep-fry thermometer.

2. Meanwhile, prepare the chicken: Pat the thighs dry, cut them into bite-sized pieces, and season with the salt and pepper. Toss them in the coconut flour until they are fully coated.

3. Working in batches of 3 or 4 pieces, fry the coated chicken in the hot oil, turning them in the oil so they cook evenly, until light brown on the outside and cooked through in the center, 3 to 5 minutes. Remove with a slotted spoon and set on a paper towel–lined plate to drain while you fry the remaining pieces.

4. Once all the chicken is cooked, make the sauce: Heat the sesame oil in a small saucepan over medium heat. Add the garlic and ginger and cook for 30 seconds, or until fragrant. Add the remaining sauce ingredients, except for the xanthan gum, and whisk to combine. Simmer for about 3 minutes, then add the xanthan gum and whisk to combine. Turn the heat up to medium-high and allow the sauce to reduce and thicken, 5 to 7 minutes.

plus oil from frying

CALORIES: 332 FAT: 15.5g PROTEIN: 35g CARBS: 13g FIBER: 6.5g SUGAR ALCOHOL: 15g

5. While the sauce reduces, steam the rice: Put the riced cauliflower in a microwave-safe bowl and cover with 2 or 3 damp paper towels. Microwave for 4 to 5 minutes, until tender but not mushy. Divide the steamed cauliflower rice between 2 bowls.

6. Add the chicken pieces to the saucepan with the thickened sauce and toss to coat them thoroughly; leave on the stovetop for 2 minutes to reheat. Divide the chicken and sauce between the bowls with the cauliflower rice and garnish with sesame seeds and sliced scallions, if desired.

—Chapter 5—

FRESH FIXIN'S

TURKEY BACON CLUB

MAKES: 1 serving   **PREP TIME:** 5 minutes (not including time to make bread)

There's something about making a sandwich with three slices of bread that brings a smile to our faces. It enables you to pack more delicious fillings in the middle. We love piling our club sandwiches high with turkey, bacon, and cheese! We don't go the traditional route with this club by toasting the bread, but feel free to toast it in a skillet on the stovetop or in the oven, if desired.

2 tablespoons mayonnaise, homemade (page 248) or store-bought

3 slices The Best Keto Bread (page 76)

2 lettuce leaves

4 slices Roma tomato

1 slice thick-cut bacon, cooked and cut in half crosswise

1 slice cheddar cheese, cut in half

3 ounces sliced turkey deli meat

1. Spread one-third of the mayo on one side of each of the bread slices.

2. Create the first layer: On one of the mayo-slathered bread slices, layer a lettuce leaf, 2 tomato slices, the bacon, and a half slice of cheese. Top that with another mayo-slathered slice of bread, mayo side facing up (this will be the middle slice).

3. Create the second layer: On top of the middle bread slice, layer the turkey and the remaining cheese, tomato slices, and lettuce.

4. Top with the third slice of bread, mayo facing down. Cut the sandwich in half or, if you'd like to stick to tradition, into quarters.

TWIST

Matt is not a fan of mayo, so he uses guacamole instead!

CALORIES: 803   FAT: 67.4g   PROTEIN: 43.8g   CARBS: 9.2g   FIBER: 3.3g

CAPRESE CHICKEN SKILLET

MAKES: 4 servings   **PREP TIME:** 10 minutes   **COOK TIME:** 15 minutes

A good caprese chicken is all about the freshness of the ingredients you use. When there are fresh cherry tomatoes and basil at our local farmers' market, we always make this dish. The key is to not overcook anything and to let the fresh flavors of the ingredients shine.

1 tablespoon extra-virgin olive oil

1 pound boneless, skinless chicken thighs

1½ teaspoons pink Himalayan salt, divided

½ teaspoon ground black pepper

1 teaspoon minced garlic

12 cherry tomatoes, halved (about 3 ounces)

¼ teaspoon red pepper flakes

1 medium-sized zucchini, spiral-sliced into noodles

3 or 4 large fresh basil leaves, minced

3 ounces mini mozzarella balls, halved

1. Heat the olive oil in a large skillet over medium-high heat.

2. Chop the chicken into 1-inch pieces and season with 1 teaspoon of the salt and the black pepper.

3. Put the chicken in the hot skillet and cook through, 5 to 7 minutes. (When fully cooked, the chicken will no longer be pink in the middle.) Remove from the skillet and set aside.

4. Turn the heat down to low and use a spatula to scrape up the drippings from the bottom of the skillet. Add the garlic and cook for 20 seconds. Add the tomatoes, remaining ½ teaspoon of salt, and red pepper flakes. Stir to combine and cover with a lid. Cook for 5 to 7 minutes, until the tomatoes have burst and softened.

5. Turn the heat back up to high, add the zucchini noodles and basil, and cook for 1 minute, until the noodles are slightly tender but not mushy. Remove from the heat, add the chicken and mozzarella, and toss to combine. Serve immediately.

NOTE

The zucchini noodles do not store and reheat well; however, if there are leftovers, they can be kept in a sealed container in the refrigerator for up to 1 day and reheated in the microwave for 30 to 60 seconds.

CALORIES: 226   FAT: 11.8g   PROTEIN: 26.3g   CARBS: 3.5g   FIBER: 1g

BAJA FISH SOFT TACOS

MAKES: 2 servings   **PREP TIME:** 15 minutes (not including time to make tortillas)
COOK TIME: 10 minutes

You don't need to be a surfer to enjoy the fresh flavors of a well-made fish taco. Sometimes we like to make these when we're trapped inside during a snowstorm to bring back memories of a relaxing day at the beach.

FISH:

1 teaspoon chili powder

1 teaspoon ground cumin

½ teaspoon pink Himalayan salt

¼ teaspoon garlic powder

¼ teaspoon onion powder

⅛ teaspoon cayenne pepper

12 ounces cod fillets

SAUCE:

½ cup sour cream

¼ cup mayonnaise, homemade (page 248) or store-bought

1 teaspoon lime juice

1 teaspoon minced fresh cilantro

1 teaspoon pink Himalayan salt

1 teaspoon chili powder

½ teaspoon ground cumin

½ teaspoon paprika

¼ teaspoon cayenne pepper

¼ teaspoon garlic powder

PICO DE GALLO:

1 small Roma tomato, diced

½ medium-sized white onion, diced

1 teaspoon lime juice

1 bunch fresh cilantro, minced

¼ teaspoon pink Himalayan salt

½ batch Coconut Flour Tortillas (page 92)

FOR SERVING:

Avocado slices (optional)

Fresh cilantro leaves (optional)

Lime wedges

NOTE

The assembled tacos should be enjoyed right away; they do not store or reheat well. (The tortillas get soggy.)

1. Preheat the oven to 400°F and line a rimmed baking sheet with parchment paper.

2. Make the fish: Put the seasonings for the fish in a small bowl and combine using a fork. Pat the fish dry with paper towels and evenly coat the fish with the seasoning mixture.

3. Lay the fish on the baking sheet and bake for 8 to 10 minutes, until opaque in the center and slightly firm to the touch. Set aside.

4. Make the sauce: Put all the ingredients for the sauce in a medium-sized mixing bowl and combine using a whisk. Set aside.

5. Make the pico de gallo: Place all the ingredients in a small bowl and stir with a spoon. Set aside.

6. Assemble the tacos: Across the middle of a tortilla, layer about one-eighth of the fish, then top with a spoonful of pico de gallo and a drizzle of sauce. Repeat until all 8 tacos are made. Top with avocado slices and cilantro leaves, if desired. Serve with lime wedges.

CALORIES: 270   FAT: 6.8g   PROTEIN: 39.8g   CARBS: 9.3g   FIBER: 4.8g

CURRY CHICKEN SALAD

MAKES: 4 servings   **PREP TIME:** 10 minutes

Chicken salad is one of our favorite things to have prepared in case we don't have time to cook a fresh meal. We have tried tons of different flavor combinations, but our favorite way to season chicken salad is with the rich and earthy flavor of curry powder!

1½ pounds boneless, skinless chicken thighs, cooked

⅓ cup mayonnaise, homemade (page 248) or store-bought

2 tablespoons sour cream

Juice of ½ lemon

1½ tablespoons minced fresh chives, plus extra for garnish

1½ teaspoons curry powder

¼ teaspoon pink Himalayan salt

¼ teaspoon ground black pepper

2 stalks celery, chopped

1. Chop the cooked chicken into bite-sized pieces and set aside.

2. Put the mayo, sour cream, lemon juice, chives, curry powder, salt, and pepper in a medium-sized mixing bowl and stir to combine.

3. Add the chicken pieces and celery to the mayo mixture and toss to coat thoroughly. Serve garnished with additional chives, if desired.

NOTE

The prep time listed above assumes that you've got some precooked chicken thighs on hand. We like to cook chicken on Sunday to add to salads or quick soups throughout the week. You can also use a rotisserie chicken from the hot section of your local grocery store! By the way, we do the same thing with eggs on Sunday: we hard-boil several to have on hand for quick breakfasts, salads, and snacks during the week.

TWIST

For additional crunch and color, Megha likes to toss in some pumpkin seeds and diced red onions!

CALORIES: 339   FAT: 14.2g   PROTEIN: 25.3g   CARBS: 2.3g   FIBER: 0.8g

LOADED COBB SALAD

MAKES: 1 serving **PREP TIME:** 10 minutes

Our favorite thing about a cobb salad is that it just barely passes as a salad. Start with a small bed of lettuce and pile it high with as many delicious toppings as possible.

4 to 5 cups chopped romaine lettuce

1 (4-ounce) boneless, skinless chicken breast, cooked and cut into strips

2 slices bacon, cooked and chopped

½ Roma tomato, diced

1 hard-boiled egg, sliced

½ ripe avocado, sliced

¼ cup shredded cheddar cheese

2 to 3 tablespoons salad dressing of choice (see Notes)

1. Put the lettuce in a large serving bowl.

2. Arrange the chicken, bacon, tomatoes, egg slices, and avocado slices on top of the lettuce, around the perimeter of the bowl. Put the shredded cheese in the middle.

3. Drizzle the dressing of your choice over the salad.

NOTES

The prep time listed above does not include the time to cook the chicken or bacon or to hard-boil an egg. We like to batch-cook chicken, bacon, and eggs on Sunday to have them on hand for adding to salads throughout the week. As a shortcut, you can use a rotisserie chicken from the hot section of your local grocery store.

Our favorite way to dress salads is to simply drizzle them with avocado oil and apple cider vinegar and toss to coat. A good ratio is about 2 tablespoons of oil to 1½ teaspoons of vinegar; adjust to your taste.

CALORIES: 778   FAT: 64g   PROTEIN: 43g   CARBS: 15g   FIBER: 10g

COCONUT SHRIMP

MAKES: 4 servings **PREP TIME:** 10 minutes **COOK TIME:** 20 minutes

When Matt's parents visited him at college, they would go out to dinner, and he would always order coconut shrimp. The first time he tried seafood with a sweet dipping sauce, it was definitely love at first bite. Try this recipe with our strawberry jam!

½ cup coconut flour

1 teaspoon pink Himalayan salt, divided

½ teaspoon ground black pepper, divided

2 large eggs

½ cup unsweetened shredded coconut

1 pound large shrimp, peeled and deveined

Coconut oil, for deep-frying

Strawberry Chia Seed Jam (page 252), for serving (optional)

NOTE

The nutritional information can't be precisely pinpointed due to the oil used for frying. We have provided information based on the shrimp itself, but the fat will vary based on the amount of oil that the shrimp absorbs.

1. Put the coconut flour, ½ teaspoon of the salt, and ¼ teaspoon of the pepper in a zip-top plastic bag and shake to combine.

2. Crack the eggs into a medium-sized bowl. Add the remaining ½ teaspoon of salt and ¼ teaspoon of pepper to the eggs and whisk to combine.

3. Put the shredded coconut in another medium-sized bowl and set all 3 battering components aside.

4. Batter the shrimp: Pat the shrimp dry using paper towels. Working in batches, toss the shrimp in the flour mixture, then dip them in the egg mixture, and then dredge them in the shredded coconut. Set the coated shrimp on a large plate.

5. Attach a deep-fry thermometer to a medium-sized saucepan and fill with enough coconut oil so that it comes halfway up the side of the pan. Heat over medium-high heat until it reaches 330°F to 350°F. Set out another large plate lined with paper towels for the fried shrimp to rest on.

6. When the oil reaches temperature, deep-fry the shrimp in batches, removing them once they have turned golden brown, about 5 minutes per batch. Set the fried shrimp on the paper towel–lined plate to soak up any excess oil. Serve immediately with strawberry jam, if desired.

7. Store in a sealed container in the refrigerator for up to 4 days. Reheat in the oven for maximum crispiness.

plus oil from frying

CALORIES: 276 **FAT:** 12.5g **PROTEIN:** 29.3g **CARBS:** 11g **FIBER:** 6.3g

FRIED RED SNAPPER

MAKES: 4 servings   **PREP TIME:** 10 minutes   **COOK TIME:** 20 minutes

This is the perfect dish if you're looking to impress your friends. We always make this along with a few other main dishes to share when we have friends over for a dinner party.

1 cup coconut flour

1 whole red snapper (about 1½ pounds)

1 cup coconut oil

½ teaspoon pink Himalayan salt

SAUCE:

2 tablespoons soy sauce

1 tablespoon toasted sesame oil

Juice of 1 lime

¼ teaspoon garlic powder

¼ teaspoon ginger powder

¼ teaspoon onion powder

¼ teaspoon paprika

¼ teaspoon ground black pepper

Lime wedges, for serving

1. Place the coconut flour in a zip-top plastic bag. Pat the snapper dry with paper towels, score the skin, and place it in the bag with the flour. Seal the bag and shake thoroughly to coat the fish. Set aside.

2. Put the coconut oil in a 12-inch or larger heavy skillet (preferably cast-iron) over medium-high heat. (Make sure the skillet is large enough to fit the fish.) Place a deep-fry thermometer in the oil and heat until it reaches 350°F.

3. Place the snapper in the hot oil and shallow-fry for 10 minutes on each side, until brown and crispy on the outside. Set aside on a large plate and season with the salt.

4. In a small bowl, whisk together the ingredients for the sauce.

5. Pour the sauce evenly over the fried snapper and serve immediately with lime wedges.

6. Store leftovers in a sealed container in the refrigerator for up to 4 days. Reheat in the microwave for a couple minutes.

NOTES

Only half of the coconut flour will adhere to the fish when you coat it in Step 1, which is reflected in the nutritional information.

The fat content can't be precisely pinpointed due to the oil used for frying. We have provided information based on the fish itself, but the fat will vary based on the amount of oil that the fish absorbs.

plus oil from frying

| CALORIES: 183 | FAT: 6g | PROTEIN: 25.5g | CARBS: 5.8g | FIBER: 2.5g |

CALIFORNIA COLLARD WRAP

MAKES: 1 serving **PREP TIME:** 10 minutes

A great option for lowering your carb intake is to sub lettuce wraps for breads and buns. Collard greens make for the sturdiest wraps and hold all those yummy toppings inside with minimal spillage.

2 large collard leaves

1 tablespoon mayonnaise, homemade (page 248) or store-bought

4 ounces sliced turkey deli meat

½ small tomato, sliced

½ avocado, sliced

2 slices cooked bacon (optional)

Pink Himalayan salt and ground black pepper

1. Cut the stalks out of both collard leaves and cut them in half lengthwise. Overlap all 4 pieces so that there are no gaps.

2. Spread the mayo down first, then layer on the turkey, tomato, avocado, and bacon, if using. Season with salt and pepper.

3. Roll the leaves halfway, tuck in the sides, and finish rolling. Cut the wrap in half and use a toothpick to stabilize it for serving, if desired.

TWIST

Matt likes to double the meat, toss in a couple slices of bacon, and drizzle with olive oil to up the fat content of this wrap!

CALORIES: 353   FAT: 23g   PROTEIN: 25g   CARBS: 10g   FIBER: 7g

STRAWBERRY COCONUT SMOOTHIE

MAKES: 1 serving   **PREP TIME:** 3 minutes

Over the past year, we've gotten into the habit of making smoothies almost daily. We usually opt for green smoothies (see page 172), but occasionally we like to treat ourselves to this more indulgent combination of strawberry and coconut. The collagen and heavy cream give it an extra-thick consistency.

3½ ounces fresh strawberries (about ¾ cup), hulled, plus extra for garnish (optional)

1 cup coconut milk, chilled

2 tablespoons heavy whipping cream

2 tablespoons unsweetened coconut flakes

1 scoop unflavored collagen peptides

¼ teaspoon liquid stevia

¼ teaspoon pink Himalayan salt

Put all the ingredients in a blender and blend until smooth, 30 to 45 seconds. Pour into a 16-ounce glass and serve immediately, garnished with strawberries, if desired.

CALORIES: 294   FAT: 23g   PROTEIN: 12g   CARBS: 13g   FIBER: 4g

GREEN POWER SMOOTHIE

MAKES: 1 serving   **PREP TIME:** 5 minutes

This smoothie is a daily staple of ours. It's a great way to load up on nutrients while getting in some high-quality fats and protein. You might be surprised by how well spinach and chocolate go together!

1 cup frozen spinach

1 cup unsweetened almond milk

2 tablespoons hemp hearts

1 tablespoon MCT oil

1 scoop chocolate-flavored protein powder

Put all the ingredients in a blender and blend until smooth, 30 to 45 seconds. Pour into a 16-ounce glass and serve immediately.

NOTES

If you are new to using MCT oil, you may want to start with 1 teaspoon and work your way up to 1 tablespoon, because MCT oil can cause digestive issues and discomfort. You can also replace the MCT oil with 2 tablespoons of heavy whipping cream.

You can use any flavor of protein powder you have on hand; just be aware that the flavor of the protein powder will dictate the flavor of the smoothie! If you use unflavored protein powder, add 12 to 15 drops of liquid stevia for equivalent sweetness.

CALORIES: 416   FAT: 27g   PROTEIN: 35g   CARBS: 7g   FIBER: 3g

RASPBERRY LIME ICE POPS

MAKES: 6 pops (1 per serving) **ACTIVE PREP TIME:** 10 minutes
INACTIVE PREP TIME: 6 hours

If you need some peace and quiet, just hand your kids one of these ice pops! They are the perfect treat for a hot summer day, and they have ingredients you can feel good about. You can use any kind of berries you want, but raspberries are our favorite for pairing with lime.

1 (13½-ounce) can coconut cream

½ cup fresh raspberries

2 tablespoons lime juice

12 drops of liquid stevia

Special equipment:
6 (4½-ounce) ice pop molds

1. Put the ingredients in a blender, reserving a few of the raspberries to put in the bottoms of the molds prior to freezing, if desired. Blend until smooth.

2. If you set aside some raspberries, roughly chop them and drop them into the molds before adding the blended mixture. Pour the mixture evenly into the molds and freeze for at least 6 hours prior to serving.

NOTE

Our ice pop mold makes 6 pops. If yours makes fewer than that, you can halve the recipe so you don't end up with leftover mixture.

CALORIES: 140 FAT: 14.2g PROTEIN: 1g CARBS: 3.3g FIBER: 0g

CANDIED GEORGIA PECANS

MAKES: 12 servings   **PREP TIME:** 10 minutes   **COOK TIME:** 1 hour

We recently moved to Atlanta, Georgia, and immediately began exploring the local farmers' markets. The first thing we purchased was a 5-pound bag of locally grown pecans. While they are great on their own, they're even better when tossed in a sweet cinnamon mixture and baked to crunchy perfection.

12 ounces raw pecan halves

1 large egg white

1 teaspoon water

2 teaspoons vanilla extract

½ teaspoon plus 10 drops of liquid stevia

1 teaspoon ground cinnamon

1 teaspoon pink Himalayan salt

1. Preheat the oven to 250°F. Line a rimmed baking sheet with parchment paper.

2. Spread the pecan halves on the prepared baking sheet in an even layer.

3. In a small bowl, whisk together the egg white, water, vanilla extract, stevia, cinnamon, and salt until combined. Pour the mixture over the pecans and toss with your hands or a spoon until the pecans are evenly coated.

4. Flatten out the pecans into a single layer and bake for 45 to 60 minutes, tossing every 15 minutes. The pecans are done when they have fully dried out and browned.

NOTE

This method can be used with the nut of your choosing!

CALORIES: 202   FAT: 24g   PROTEIN: 3.3g   CARBS: 4.2g   FIBER: 3.1g

FATHEAD CRACKERS

MAKES: 8 servings   **PREP TIME:** 10 minutes   **COOK TIME:** 10 minutes

When starting a keto diet, the first things a lot of people miss are chips and crackers. The crunch factor! These fathead crackers will fill that void.

1½ cups shredded mozzarella cheese (about 6 ounces)

2 ounces cream cheese (¼ cup)

1 cup blanched almond flour

1 large egg

½ teaspoon dried parsley

½ teaspoon pink Himalayan salt

TWIST

Give the crackers a kick with some minced garlic and chili powder!

1. Preheat the oven to 425°F and line a baking sheet with parchment paper.

2. Put the mozzarella and cream cheese in a large microwave-safe mixing bowl and microwave for 30 seconds. Combine using a rubber spatula. Microwave for another 30 seconds, until the cheese has melted, then stir once more.

3. Add the almond flour, egg, parsley, and salt and, using a fork, combine everything thoroughly until you have a soft, sticky, and pliable dough.

4. Once the dough comes together, transfer it to the lined baking sheet and place another piece of parchment paper on top. Roll out into a thin rectangle, about ¼ inch thick. Using a pizza cutter or knife, cut the flattened dough into 20 to 25 small crackers, about 1 inch.

5. Discard any extra dough and spread out the crackers so they are not touching one another. Bake for 7 to 10 minutes, until the crackers have puffed up and browned. Allow to cool on the baking sheet for 10 minutes prior to eating.

6. These are best eaten the same day they are baked, but leftovers can be stored in a sealed container in the refrigerator for up to 5 days. To recrisp, place in a preheated 250°F oven for 5 minutes; however, they will not get as crispy as when freshly baked.

CALORIES: 174   **FAT:** 14.6g   **PROTEIN:** 9.4g   **CARBS:** 4g   **FIBER:** 1.5g

MEXICAN LAYER DIP ⊘ ⊘

MAKES: 16 servings **ACTIVE PREP TIME:** 25 minutes **INACTIVE PREP TIME:** 2 to 3 hours
COOK TIME: 8 minutes

Who doesn't love digging into a delicious layer dip while lying on the couch watching football? This recipe is a favorite of ours during football season. The worse our favorite teams do, the more dip we tend to eat.

LAYER 1 (BEEF AND BEANS):

8 ounces ground beef (80/20)

1 (4-ounce) can green chilies

½ (15-ounce) can black soybeans, drained

½ teaspoon pink Himalayan salt

¼ teaspoon ground black pepper

LAYER 2 (SEASONED SOUR CREAM):

1 cup sour cream

1 teaspoon dried oregano leaves

¾ teaspoon garlic powder

¾ teaspoon ground cumin

¾ teaspoon paprika

½ teaspoon chili powder

½ teaspoon pink Himalayan salt

LAYER 3 (GUACAMOLE):

3 ripe avocados, peeled and pitted

1 teaspoon lime juice

½ teaspoon pink Himalayan salt

½ teaspoon ground black pepper

¼ teaspoon ground cumin

¼ small red onion, diced (optional)

LAYER 4 (CHEESE):

1 cup shredded Mexican cheese blend (about 4 ounces)

LAYER 5 (PICO DE GALLO):

1 Roma tomato, diced

½ small white onion, diced

½ teaspoon lime juice

¼ teaspoon pink Himalayan salt

2 tablespoons minced fresh cilantro

FOR SERVING:

Crackers, homemade (page 180) or store-bought

1. Make layer 1: Heat a medium-sized skillet over medium-high heat and spray with coconut oil spray. Put the ground beef in the hot skillet and cook through, stirring to break up the meat as it cooks, about 8 minutes.

2. Add the green chilies, soybeans, salt, and pepper and stir to combine. Layer in the bottom of a 7-quart glass baking dish.

3. Make layer 2: In a bowl, whisk together the layer 2 ingredients. Dollop onto the meat and bean mixture in the baking dish and spread evenly using a rubber spatula.

4. Make layer 3: In a medium-sized bowl, mash the avocados using a fork. Add the lime juice, salt, pepper, and cumin and combine with the fork. Mix in the diced red onion, if using. Dollop on top of the sour cream mixture in the baking dish and spread evenly using the spatula.

5. Add layer 4: Sprinkle the cheese blend evenly over the guacamole layer in the baking dish.

CALORIES: 159   **FAT:** 12.8g   **PROTEIN:** 6.6g   **CARBS:** 5.6g   **FIBER:** 3g

6. Make layer 5: Put the diced tomato and onion in a small bowl. Add the lime juice and toss using a spoon. Add the salt and cilantro and toss once more.

7. Layer the pico de gallo over the shredded cheese and chill the dip for 2 to 3 hours before serving.

8. Store in a sealed container in the refrigerator for up to 4 days.

BUFFALO CHICKEN DIP ⌀ 🥜 👍

MAKES: 16 servings   **PREP TIME:** 5 minutes   **COOK TIME:** 20 minutes

How do you eat Buffalo wings without getting all messy? Turn the wings into a creamy dip and serve it with celery sticks!

12 ounces cream cheese (1½ cups)

¾ cup Frank's RedHot sauce

3 cups cooked and shredded chicken breast

¾ cup blue cheese dressing, preferably homemade (see Note)

1 cup shredded mozzarella cheese (about 4 ounces), divided

¼ cup sliced jalapeños

Celery sticks, for serving

1. Preheat the oven to 350°F.

2. Put the cream cheese and hot sauce in a medium-sized saucepan over medium heat. As the cream cheese begins to melt, stir the cheese and hot sauce until combined.

3. Once the cream cheese is fully melted, add the chicken and blue cheese dressing and stir to coat the chicken in the sauce. Turn off the heat and stir in ¾ cup of the mozzarella cheese.

4. Transfer the mixture to an 8-inch round baking pan and layer the rest of the mozzarella and the jalapeños on top. Bake for 10 minutes, until the cheese is melted and bubbling. Serve with celery sticks.

5. Store leftovers in a sealed container in the refrigerator for up to 5 days. Reheat in the microwave for a couple minutes.

TIP

We make this recipe time and time again for parties and on game days. A great tip to speed up the prep time is to use a rotisserie chicken from the hot section of your grocery store!

NOTE

Store-bought blue cheese dressings usually contain soybean oil. For this recipe, which calls for a lot of dressing, we recommend that you use homemade. To whip some up easily, simply combine equal parts avocado oil–based mayo and sour cream, add crumbled blue cheese, and thin with a little lemon juice.

CALORIES: 183   FAT: 13.8g   PROTEIN: 11.9g   CARBS: 1.8g   FIBER: 0g

SWEET AND SPICY BEEF JERKY

MAKES: 16 servings **ACTIVE PREP TIME:** 15 minutes
INACTIVE PREP TIME: 4 to 24 hours **COOK TIME:** 4 to 6 hours

This jerky is our favorite keto snack. We make it about once a month and store it in the fridge for a guilt-free grab-and-go option. The apple cider vinegar balances out the heat of the hot sauce to make this jerky irresistibly sweet and spicy.

3 pounds flat-iron steak

MARINADE:

½ cup soy sauce

½ cup apple cider vinegar

¼ cup Frank's RedHot sauce

½ teaspoon liquid stevia

2 teaspoons liquid smoke

2 teaspoons ground black pepper

1½ teaspoons garlic powder

1 teaspoon onion powder

Special equipment:

10 (12-inch) bamboo skewers

NOTE

Three pounds of raw meat will yield one pound of jerky.

1. Marinate the steak: Slice the steak into thin jerky-sized strips, about ¼ inch thick, and put them in a gallon-sized zip-top plastic bag. Add the marinade ingredients, seal the bag, and shake to fully coat the meat.

2. Seal the bag tightly (removing any excess air) and place it in a bowl to catch any leakage. Place the bowl in the refrigerator for at least 4 hours or up to 24 hours.

3. Make the jerky: Adjust the racks in your oven so that one is in the highest position and one is in the lowest position. Preheat the oven to 190°F.

4. Remove the steak strips from the marinade and pat them as dry as possible using paper towels; discard the remaining marinade.

5. Using bamboo skewers, pierce the tip of each meat strip so that there are anywhere from 5 to 7 strips hanging on each skewer. Be sure to leave space between the strips so that air can circulate around them. Hang the skewers from the top oven rack and place a rimmed baking sheet on the lowest rack to catch any drippings.

6. Bake for 4 to 6 hours, until the jerky is dry to the touch.

7. Store in a zip-top plastic bag in the refrigerator for up to 10 days.

CALORIES: 150   FAT: 9.8g   PROTEIN: 15.8g   CARBS: 0.5g   FIBER: 0g

CHARLIE'S ENERGY BALLS

MAKES: 20 balls (1 per serving)   **PREP TIME:** 10 minutes   **COOK TIME:** 20 minutes

This recipe is an ode to Charlie Kelly from the TV show *It's Always Sunny in Philadelphia*. In one episode, he goes on a three-day video gaming binge and is fueled by "energy balls." This is our take on Charlie's energy balls. We use these as a quick fuel source when we're out and about.

½ cup natural almond butter, room temperature

¼ cup coconut oil, melted

1 large egg

½ cup coconut flour

2 tablespoons unflavored beef gelatin powder

1 scoop chocolate-flavored whey protein powder

1. Preheat the oven to 350°F and grease a rimmed baking sheet with coconut oil spray.

2. In a large mixing bowl, mix together the almond butter, coconut oil, and egg using a fork. In a small bowl, whisk together the coconut flour, gelatin, and protein powder.

3. Pour the dry ingredients into the wet mixture and mash with a fork until you have a cohesive dough. It should not be too sticky. *Note:* If the dough doesn't come together well or is very sticky, add a little coconut flour until it combines well.

4. Using your hands, form the dough into 20 even-sized balls, about 1½ inches in diameter, and put them on the prepared baking sheet.

5. Bake for 20 minutes, until slightly browned and hardened. Allow to cool on the baking sheet for 10 minutes prior to serving.

6. Store in a zip-top plastic bag in the refrigerator for up to a week.

CALORIES: 91   FAT: 7.1g   PROTEIN: 4.1g   CARBS: 3g   FIBER: 1.6g

BAR SIDE MOZZARELLA STICKS

MAKES: 16 sticks (4 per serving) **ACTIVE PREP TIME:** 20 minutes
INACTIVE PREP TIME: 2 hours **COOK TIME:** 20 minutes

We're convinced that the most delicious foods are the ones found on kids' menus. Who says we can't enjoy kids' menu foods as adults? Let's reclaim the kids' menu together, starting with mozzarella sticks!

3 ounces pork rinds, finely ground

¼ cup grated Parmesan cheese, plus extra for garnish

½ teaspoon dried oregano leaves

½ teaspoon red pepper flakes

½ teaspoon pink Himalayan salt

½ teaspoon ground black pepper

2 large eggs

1 tablespoon heavy whipping cream

8 sticks mozzarella string cheese

2 cups coconut oil, for deep-frying

Low-carb marinara sauce, for serving (optional)

1. Place the pork rinds, Parmesan, oregano, red pepper flakes, salt, and pepper in a shallow dish and combine with a fork.

2. Place the eggs and cream in a separate shallow dish and lightly beat with a fork.

3. Cut each stick of string cheese in half crosswise. Dip each piece in the egg mixture and then in the pork rind mixture. Make sure that each piece has a thick coating. You may have to press the breading into the cheese to ensure an even coat. Place on a plate and freeze for 2 hours.

4. In a 2-quart saucepan, heat the oil over medium-high heat until it reaches between 330°F and 345°F on a deep-fry thermometer.

5. Remove the breaded cheese sticks from the freezer. Fry in batches for 3 to 5 minutes per batch, until golden brown. Use a slotted spoon to remove the sticks from the oil and place on a paper towel–lined plate to drain. Allow to cool for 5 minutes, then garnish with grated Parmesan. Serve with marinara sauce, if desired.

6. Store leftovers in a sealed container in the refrigerator for up to 4 days. Reheat in a preheated 350°F oven for 10 minutes.

NOTE

The nutritional information can't be precisely pinpointed due to the oil used for frying. We have provided information based on the cheese sticks themselves, but the fat content will vary based on the amount of oil the cheese sticks absorb.

plus oil from frying

| CALORIES: 356 | FAT: 25.2g | PROTEIN: 31.6g | CARBS: 2.4g | FIBER: 0g |

SALAMI CHIPS WITH PESTO

MAKES: 6 servings **PREP TIME:** 10 minutes **COOK TIME:** 12 minutes

Anytime we can get our hands on some fresh basil, we always rush home and make a big batch of pesto. It's a great high-fat sauce that pairs well with lots of different dishes. For a late-night snack, we often crisp up some salami chips and load them up with pesto!

CHIPS:

6 ounces sliced Genoa salami

PESTO:

1 cup fresh basil leaves

3 cloves garlic

¼ cup grated Parmesan cheese

¼ cup raw walnuts

¼ teaspoon pink Himalayan salt

¼ teaspoon ground black pepper

½ cup extra-virgin olive oil

1. Make the chips: Preheat the oven to 375°F and line 2 rimmed baking sheets with parchment paper.

2. Arrange the salami in a single layer on the lined baking sheets. Bake for 10 to 12 minutes, until crisp. Transfer to a paper towel–lined plate to absorb the excess oil. Allow to cool and crisp up further.

3. Make the pesto: Put all the pesto ingredients, except for the olive oil, in a food processor and pulse until everything is roughly chopped and a coarse paste has formed.

4. With the food processor running, slowly pour in the olive oil. Process until all of the oil has been added and the ingredients are fully incorporated. Taste and season with additional salt and pepper, if desired.

5. Pour the pesto into a small serving bowl and serve the salami chips alongside. Store leftover pesto in a sealed container in the refrigerator for up to 2 weeks; store the chips in a zip-top plastic bag in the refrigerator for up to 5 days.

TWIST

When we have pine nuts in the pantry, Matt prefers to replace the walnuts in this recipe with pine nuts.

CALORIES: 202   **FAT:** 9.4g   **PROTEIN:** 7.5g   **CARBS:** 1.2g   **FIBER:** 0.1g

RADICAL RADISH CHIPS

MAKES: 2 servings **PREP TIME:** 10 minutes **COOK TIME:** 20 minutes

Believe us, we've tried turning literally every low-carb vegetable into chips. Most of them were complete fails, but these radish chips were a standout winner. The bigger the radishes you can find, the bigger the chips you can make.

1 (16-ounce) bag radishes

1½ cups coconut oil, for deep-frying

¾ teaspoon pink Himalayan salt

½ teaspoon ground black pepper

1. Using a sharp knife, cut the root ends off the radishes, then slice the radishes into thin chips. Place in a bowl and set aside.

2. Heat the coconut oil in a medium-sized saucepan over medium-high heat until the temperature reaches between 330°F and 350°F on a deep-fry thermometer.

3. Once the oil reaches temperature, drop in 7 to 10 chips at a time, flipping them with tongs when their edges start to curl. Once they begin to brown, remove them from the oil and set on a paper towel–lined plate to absorb any excess oil.

4. Once all the chips are fried, season with the salt and pepper. Toss to coat and enjoy immediately!

NOTE

The nutritional information can't be precisely pinpointed due to the oil used for frying. We have provided information based on the chips themselves, but the fat content will vary based on the amount of oil the chips absorb.

TWIST

Megha likes to dip these chips in a simple combination of sour cream and Sriracha, a dip she's been using to coat all her foods lately!

plus oil from frying

CALORIES: 37   **FAT:** 0g   **PROTEIN:** 1.5g   **CARBS:** 7.5g   **FIBER:** 3.5g

CHEESY BROCCOLI AND BACON

MAKES: 4 servings   **PREP TIME:** 10 minutes   **COOK TIME:** 25 minutes

The best way to get your veggies in is by pairing them with bacon and cheese! This dish is great because broccoli is the perfect veggie for soaking up all the great flavors you throw at it.

4 slices bacon

5 cups fresh broccoli florets

1 teaspoon minced garlic

SAUCE:

1 tablespoon unsalted butter

2 tablespoons heavy whipping cream

1 cup shredded cheddar cheese (about 4 ounces), divided

1. Preheat the oven to 400°F.

2. Heat a medium-sized skillet over medium-high heat. Cut the bacon into bite-sized pieces and put them in the hot pan. Allow to cook through, 3 to 5 minutes. Take one-quarter of the bacon pieces out of the pan and set aside on a plate.

3. Add the broccoli and garlic to the skillet and toss to coat in the fat. Sauté for 5 to 7 minutes, until the broccoli is bright green and tender. Transfer the broccoli mixture to an 8-inch round or square baking pan or dish.

4. Make the sauce: Put the butter and cream in a small saucepan over low heat. Allow the butter to melt, stirring often.

5. Once the butter is fully melted, add ½ cup of the shredded cheese and continue to stir until the cheese has melted and formed a thick sauce.

6. Pour the sauce over the broccoli and toss to coat using a spoon. Layer the remaining ½ cup of shredded cheese and the reserved bacon over the entire mixture.

7. Bake for 10 minutes, or until the cheese has melted and slightly browned. Serve immediately.

8. Store leftovers in a sealed container in the refrigerator for up to 4 days. Reheat in the microwave for a couple minutes, until the cheese has melted.

CALORIES: 241   **FAT:** 18.5g   **PROTEIN:** 13g   **CARBS:** 8.5g   **FIBER:** 3g

HUSH PUPPIES

MAKES: 4 servings **PREP TIME:** 10 minutes **COOK TIME:** 30 minutes

Growing up, Matt's family would always take trips to the East Coast, and he's convinced that it was just for the seafood. Sure, they hit a few historic sites along the way, but really it was all about the crab, scallops, lobster, and (his personal favorite) hush puppies. Nothing goes with a fish fry or crab bake like a big basket of hush puppies.

½ cup coconut flour

¼ cup psyllium husk powder

1 teaspoon baking powder

½ teaspoon onion powder

½ teaspoon pink Himalayan salt

4 large eggs

⅓ cup extra-virgin olive oil

⅓ cup water

2 tablespoons diced white onions

Coconut oil, for deep-frying

TIP

We like to serve these hush puppies with a spicy mayo made of mayonnaise and Sriracha sauce!

1. In a small mixing bowl, combine the coconut flour, psyllium husk powder, baking powder, onion powder, and salt using a whisk. Set aside.

2. In a large mixing bowl, whisk together the eggs, olive oil, and water. Add the dry mixture to the wet mixture and mix with a wooden spoon until you have a thick, slightly sticky, and pliable dough. Fold in the diced onions using a rubber spatula.

3. Place a sheet of parchment paper on a large plate. Using your hands, form the dough into 20 even-sized balls, 1 to 1½ inches in diameter, and place on the plate.

4. Set a medium-sized saucepan over medium-high heat. Put enough coconut oil in the pan so that it is deep enough to completely submerge the hush puppies (but, for safety, do not fill the pan more than halfway full of oil). Place a deep-fry thermometer into the oil as it heats. Line a plate with paper towels.

5. When the oil temperature reaches anywhere from 330°F to 350°F, drop some of the hush puppies into the oil and fry until dark brown on the outside, about 8 minutes. Once cooked through, remove the hush puppies from the oil using a slotted spoon and place on the paper towel–lined plate to absorb the excess oil.

6. Repeat until all the hush puppies are fried. Serve immediately.

7. Store leftovers in a zip-top plastic bag. Reheat in the microwave for 30 to 60 seconds.

plus oil from frying

CALORIES: 322   **FAT:** 24.5g   **PROTEIN:** 8.3g   **CARBS:** 17g   **FIBER:** 12g

ASPARAGUS WITH GOAT CHEESE AND SUNFLOWER SEEDS

MAKES: 4 servings   **PREP TIME:** 5 minutes   **COOK TIME:** 12 minutes

In 2015, we moved from San Francisco, where we met, to Philadelphia. On one of our last nights in town, we went to a fancy steakhouse and ordered a bone-in filet mignon. To our surprise, our favorite dish of the night wasn't the steak, but a perfectly cooked asparagus dish topped with tangy goat cheese and crunchy sunflower seeds. Whenever we fall in love with a dish at a restaurant, we always have to re-create it at home.

1 bunch asparagus (about 1 pound), tough ends removed

1 tablespoon extra-virgin olive oil

½ teaspoon pink Himalayan salt

¼ teaspoon ground black pepper

2 ounces fresh (soft) goat cheese

¼ cup raw sunflower kernels

1. Preheat the oven to 400°F.

2. Line a rimmed baking sheet with a single layer of asparagus. Brush the asparagus with the olive oil and season with the salt and pepper.

3. Bake for 10 to 12 minutes, until bright green and fork-tender.

4. Crumble the goat cheese down the center of the asparagus and top with the sunflower kernels. Serve immediately.

NOTE

The cook time may vary depending on the thickness of your asparagus stalks. Our stalks were ½ inch thick at the bottom and cooked through well in the time indicated above.

CALORIES: 148   FAT: 10.1g   PROTEIN: 7.5g   CARBS: 6.3g   FIBER: 2.5g

CHIPOTLE CAULIFLOWER MASH

MAKES: 2 servings **PREP TIME:** 10 minutes **COOK TIME:** 15 minutes

If you've never tried it before, cauliflower mash is even creamier and more flavorful than mashed potatoes. Chipotle chili peppers give this dish some heat and a greater depth of flavor.

½ head cauliflower, cored and cut into florets

1 tablespoon unsalted butter

¼ teaspoon minced garlic

2 tablespoons heavy whipping cream

1 chipotle pepper in adobo sauce, minced (see Note)

1½ teaspoons adobo sauce (from the can of chipotle peppers, above)

½ teaspoon pink Himalayan salt

1. Fill a medium-sized saucepan halfway full of water and bring to a boil over high heat. Drop in the cauliflower florets and boil for 15 minutes, until fork-tender.

2. Drain the cauliflower and put it in a food processor. Pulse for 30 seconds.

3. Melt the butter and garlic in a small microwave-safe bowl for 30 seconds. Add the garlic butter and the cream to the food processor. Pulse until smooth. You may have to stop and scrape down the sides with a rubber spatula while processing.

4. Add the chipotle pepper, adobo sauce, and salt and process once more, until fully incorporated. Transfer to a serving bowl and serve immediately.

5. Store leftovers in a sealed container in the refrigerator for up to 4 days. Reheat in the microwave for 60 to 90 seconds.

NOTE

Chipotle peppers in adobo sauce typically come in 7-ounce cans and usually can be found in the ethnic food section of the grocery store. If you prefer more heat, you can mix more chipotle pepper and adobo sauce into the cauliflower.

CALORIES: 144   FAT: 11g   PROTEIN: 3.5g   CARBS: 9g   FIBER: 3.5g

CILANTRO LIME RICE

MAKES: 4 servings **PREP TIME:** 10 minutes **COOK TIME:** 10 minutes

Miracle Rice is a low-carb option that we use all the time. On its own, it is flavorless, but it's great for piling high with sauces and seasonings. This cilantro lime–flavored rice is a great side for Mexican dishes.

3 (8-ounce) packages Miracle Rice (see Note)

3 tablespoons unsalted butter

1½ teaspoons minced garlic

Juice of 1 lime

1 teaspoon pink Himalayan salt

½ teaspoon ground black pepper

3 tablespoons chopped fresh cilantro

Lime wedges, for serving (optional)

1. Put the rice in a fine-mesh sieve or a colander with small holes and rinse with hot water.

2. Heat a large skillet over medium heat. Put the rice in the hot skillet and, stirring continuously, allow most of the liquid to evaporate, 5 to 7 minutes.

3. When nearly all of the liquid has evaporated, add the butter and garlic and stir until the butter is melted and the rice is coated in the butter. Add the lime juice, salt, and pepper and stir to combine. Cook for 2 more minutes, until the lime juice has evaporated.

4. Stir in the cilantro and serve immediately, with lime wedges on the side, if desired.

5. Store leftovers in a sealed container in the refrigerator for up to 4 days. Reheat in the microwave for a couple minutes.

NOTE

We purchase Miracle Rice on Amazon in bulk because we have yet to see it at a local grocery store.

CALORIES: 90   FAT: 8.3g   PROTEIN: 0g   CARBS: 3g   FIBER: 1g

Chapter 7

DECADENT DESSERTS

CHOCOLATE PROTEIN TRUFFLES

MAKES: 6 truffles (1 per serving) **ACTIVE PREP TIME:** 10 minutes
INACTIVE PREP TIME: 30 minutes

We are huge fans of the "healthy dessert" concept, and this healthy dessert is one of our favorites. These rich, dark chocolate truffles pack some protein. They are best consumed after dinner or when your significant other isn't looking.

¼ cup blanched almond flour

2 tablespoons chocolate-flavored whey protein powder

1½ tablespoons cocoa powder

1 tablespoon natural almond butter

1 tablespoon sugar-free maple syrup

1 tablespoon unsweetened almond milk

¼ cup unsweetened coconut flakes

1. Put all the ingredients, except for the coconut flakes, in a medium-sized mixing bowl and combine with a fork until uniform in texture. Cover and refrigerate until firm to the touch, at least 30 minutes.

2. Meanwhile, chop up the coconut flakes and set aside.

3. Remove the truffle mixture from the refrigerator and roll between your hands into 6 even-sized balls, about 1½ inches in diameter. Roll the balls, one at a time, in the chopped coconut and set on a plate.

4. Store in a sealed container in the refrigerator for up to a week.

NOTE

If you use unflavored whey protein powder, we recommend that you sweeten the truffles with 10 to 12 drops of liquid stevia.

CALORIES: 83   FAT: 6.2g   PROTEIN: 4.3g   CARBS: 3.5g   FIBER: 1g   SUGAR ALCOHOL: 1.2g

DEATH BY CHOCOLATE CHEESECAKE

MAKES: one 9-inch cheesecake (12 servings) **ACTIVE PREP TIME:** 20 minutes
INACTIVE PREP TIME: 3 hours **COOK TIME:** 70 minutes

With its thick chocolaty crust and intense and creamy dark chocolate filling, this decadent cheesecake packs a whole lot of chocolate into every bite. It is so good that even your non-keto friends and family members will want the recipe! We highly recommend that you make this dessert if you want to impress that special someone (like Matt did for Megha on their first Valentine's Day together!).

CRUST:

½ cup coconut flour

½ cup cocoa powder

½ cup powdered erythritol

½ cup (1 stick) unsalted butter, melted

FILLING:

3 (8-ounce) packages cream cheese, room temperature

¼ cup plus 2 tablespoons heavy whipping cream

3 large eggs

¾ cup powdered erythritol

3 tablespoons cocoa powder

1 teaspoon vanilla extract

4 ounces unsweetened baking chocolate (100% cacao)

1 tablespoon unsalted butter

FOR GARNISH (OPTIONAL):

1 ounce unsweetened baking chocolate (100% cacao)

1. Make the crust: Preheat the oven to 350°F. Grease a 9-inch springform pan with coconut oil spray.

2. Put the coconut flour, cocoa powder, and erythritol in a medium-sized mixing bowl and combine using a fork. Pour the melted butter over the dry mixture and combine thoroughly using a rubber spatula.

3. Transfer the crust mixture to the greased pan and press into an even layer across the bottom. Par-bake the crust for 12 minutes.

4. Remove the crust from the oven and lower the oven temperature to 300°F. Allow the crust to cool for at least 20 minutes before adding the filling.

5. Make the filling: Put the cream cheese and cream in a large mixing bowl and beat with a hand mixer until combined and smooth. Add the eggs, erythritol, cocoa powder, and vanilla extract and combine with the mixer.

6. Roughly chop the 4 ounces of chocolate and put it in a microwave-safe bowl with the tablespoon of butter. Microwave in 20-second increments, stirring after each increment, until melted. (Alternatively, melt the chocolate and butter in a small heavy-bottomed saucepan on the stovetop over low heat.)

7. Add the melted chocolate mixture to the rest of the filling ingredients and mix with the hand mixer until smooth and

CALORIES: 398 FAT: 37g PROTEIN: 7.1g CARBS: 10.8g FIBER: 5.5g SUGAR ALCOHOL: 20g

NOTES

The amount of unsweetened chocolate used in the filling can be changed to your taste. For us, 4 ounces results in the perfect dark chocolate cheesecake. Cut that amount in half for a less-intense chocolate flavor.

The crust can be made a day in advance and stored in the refrigerator.

fully incorporated. Pour the filling over the cooled crust and spread evenly with the rubber spatula.

8. Bake the cheesecake for 55 minutes, until a toothpick inserted in the middle comes out clean. Set on a wire baking rack and allow to cool for 15 minutes, then place in the refrigerator until completely set, at least 3 hours.

9. Use a grater or vegetable peeler to grate or shave 1 ounce of chocolate on top of the chilled cheesecake, if desired. Allow to sit at room temperature for 30 minutes prior to serving.

10. To serve, run a knife around the edges to loosen the cheesecake, then remove the rim of the springform pan. Cut into 12 slices. Store in the refrigerator for up to a week or in the freezer for up to 3 months.

NO-CHURN PEANUT BUTTER ICE CREAM

MAKES: roughly 3 cups (½ cup per serving)   **ACTIVE PREP TIME:** 15 minutes
INACTIVE PREP TIME: 4 hours   **COOK TIME:** 12 minutes

Everyone needs a scoop of ice cream now and then, and this version using natural, creamy peanut butter is our favorite. We like to take it out of the freezer about ten minutes before we scoop it to maximize the creaminess.

2 cups heavy whipping cream

3 tablespoons unsalted butter, plus extra for topping (optional)

⅔ cup powdered erythritol

4 large egg yolks

2 tablespoons natural creamy peanut butter, plus extra for topping (optional)

1 teaspoon vanilla extract

⅛ teaspoon xanthan gum

NOTE

This recipe calls for consuming raw eggs, which we are comfortable doing. If you are concerned, feel free to use pasteurized eggs.

TWIST

Matt likes to make this ice cream using almond butter instead of peanut butter to change up the flavor!

1. Put the cream, butter, and erythritol in a medium-sized heavy-bottomed saucepan over medium-high heat. Mix using a whisk until the sweetener has dissolved. Bring to a boil, then lower the heat and simmer rapidly for 5 to 7 minutes, until slightly thickened. Remove from the heat and let cool for about 15 minutes, until just warm to the touch.

2. Put the egg yolks in a large mixing bowl and mix using a hand mixer until lightened to a pale yellow color, 30 to 45 seconds. Add the peanut butter and vanilla extract and combine with the mixer.

3. Slowly add the cooled cream mixture to the egg yolk mixture while mixing with the hand mixer. Add the xanthan gum and continue to mix until a frothy layer has formed on the top.

4. Pour the ice cream mixture into an 8 by 4-inch loaf pan and place in the freezer for 30 minutes. Mix with a spoon, then return the pan to the freezer for another 30 minutes. Mix again, then return the pan to the freezer until the ice cream is hard enough to scoop, at least 3 more hours.

5. Allow the ice cream to sit out at room temperature for 10 minutes prior to serving. If desired, garnish each serving with a spoonful of peanut butter or with a quick peanut butter drizzle (as shown in the photo), made by combining equal parts peanut butter and butter in a microwave-safe bowl, microwaving until the butter has melted, and then combining them with a spoon until smooth.

6. Store in a sealed container in the freezer for up to a week.

CALORIES: 392   FAT: 40.5g   PROTEIN: 4.8g   CARBS: 3.7g   FIBER: 0.5g   SUGAR ALCOHOL: 21g

SNICKERDOODLE CREAM CHEESECAKE

MAKES: 1 serving **ACTIVE PREP TIME:** 5 minutes
INACTIVE PREP TIME: 30 minutes **COOK TIME:** 90 seconds

Microwave cakes are our absolute favorite keto desserts. We aren't the most patient people, so the fact that we can whip up this snickerdoodle cake in under five minutes is perfect. And who doesn't love cutting into a surprise cream cheese filling?

FILLING:

1 tablespoon cream cheese, room temperature

1 teaspoon powdered erythritol

1 teaspoon ground cinnamon

CAKE:

1½ tablespoons coconut flour

1 tablespoon golden flax meal

¼ teaspoon baking powder

⅛ teaspoon cream of tartar

2 tablespoons unsalted butter, melted but not hot

1 large egg

½ teaspoon vanilla extract

¼ teaspoon plus 15 drops of liquid stevia

FOR GARNISH (OPTIONAL):

Ground cinnamon

Powdered erythritol

1. Make the filling: Place a piece of plastic wrap in a small bowl and put the cream cheese, erythritol, and cinnamon in the center. Use a spoon to combine the ingredients, then wrap the plastic wrap around the mixture to enclose it securely. Using your hands, form the filling into a small disc, 1 inch in diameter and ½ inch thick. Place in the freezer for 30 minutes.

2. Make the cake: In a small bowl, use a fork to whisk together the coconut flour, flax meal, baking powder, and cream of tartar. In another small bowl, whisk together the melted butter, egg, vanilla extract, and stevia.

3. Slowly add the dry mixture to the wet mixture and whisk together until it has a thick batterlike consistency.

4. Grease a 4- or 5-ounce microwave-safe ramekin with coconut oil spray. Pour half of the batter into the ramekin. Remove the cream cheese disc from the freezer, unwrap, and place in the center of the ramekin. Gently press it down, but do not let it hit the bottom. Pour the rest of the batter on top of the filling and spread, fully covering the disc and creating an even surface.

5. Microwave for 90 seconds. Flip the cake over onto a plate and, if desired, dust with ground cinnamon and powdered erythritol. Enjoy!

NOTE

If you prefer, you can bake the cake at 350°F for 25 minutes.

CALORIES: 403 FAT: 36g PROTEIN: 11g CARBS: 12g FIBER: 7g SUGAR ALCOHOL: 4g

GIANT SKILLET COOKIE FOR TWO

MAKES: 6-inch cookie (2 servings)   PREP TIME: 10 minutes   COOK TIME: 20 minutes

This is the perfect date-night dessert! When we finish dinner and can feel a snack-fest coming on, we clean the kitchen, put on some music, and make this giant skillet cookie together. It's always better to have a delicious dessert that you put some thought and effort into than to snack mindlessly. You can wait for the cookie to cool completely and then cut it into slices, or dig in with a spoon as soon as it comes out of the oven.

½ cup blanched almond flour

1 teaspoon unflavored beef gelatin powder

½ teaspoon baking powder

¼ teaspoon pink Himalayan salt

2 tablespoons unsalted butter

1 tablespoon cream cheese

2 tablespoons heavy whipping cream

1 large egg yolk

½ teaspoon vanilla extract

½ teaspoon liquid stevia

2 tablespoons sugar-free chocolate chips, divided

1. Preheat the oven to 350°F and grease a 6-inch oven-safe skillet with coconut oil spray.

2. In a small bowl, combine the almond flour, gelatin, baking powder, and salt using a fork. Set aside.

3. Put the butter and cream cheese in a small microwave-safe bowl that's large enough to accommodate the beaters of a hand mixer. Microwave for 20 to 30 seconds, just until soft. Combine using a hand mixer. Add the cream, egg yolk, vanilla extract, and stevia and mix to combine.

4. Add the dry mixture to the wet mixture and combine using the mixer until uniform. Fold in 1½ tablespoons of the chocolate chips using a rubber spatula.

5. Pour the mixture into the greased skillet and spread evenly with the spatula. Top the cookie with the remaining ½ tablespoon of chocolate chips. Bake for 20 minutes, or until golden brown.

6. Allow to rest in the skillet for 15 minutes prior to serving, or dig in immediately with spoons, if desired.

TWIST

Matt likes to add walnuts to his half of the cookie for crunch and flavor!

CALORIES: 406   FAT: 38.5g   PROTEIN: 9.5g   CARBS: 11.2g   FIBER: 4.5g   SUGAR ALCOHOL: 2.3g

FLOURLESS CHOCOLATE CAKE

MAKES: one 9-inch cake (8 servings)   PREP TIME: 10 minutes   COOK TIME: 42 minutes

Are you a dark chocolate fan? This recipe uses 100 percent cacao chocolate for a truly intense dark chocolate flavor. One slice and your chocolate craving will be satisfied.

5 ounces unsweetened baking chocolate (100% cacao)

½ cup (1 stick) plus 2 tablespoons unsalted butter

5 large eggs

1 cup powdered erythritol

½ cup cocoa powder

½ teaspoon baking powder

1. Preheat the oven to 350°F and grease a 9-inch springform pan with coconut oil spray.

2. Put the chocolate and butter in a small microwave-safe bowl and microwave for 30 seconds. Stir and microwave for another 30 seconds, then stir again. If the chocolate is not fully melted, continue to microwave in 20- to 30-second intervals, stirring after each interval. Set aside.

3. Crack the eggs into a large bowl and mix with a hand mixer until frothy. Slowly pour in the melted chocolate as you keep mixing. Set aside.

4. Put the erythritol, cocoa powder, and baking powder in a small bowl and combine using a fork. In 2 batches, add the dry mixture to the wet mixture and combine using the mixer until you have a thick batter.

5. Pour the batter into the greased springform pan and bake for 40 minutes, or until a toothpick inserted in the center of the cake comes out clean. Allow to rest in the pan for 15 minutes prior to cutting and serving. To serve, run a knife around the edges to loosen the cake, then remove the rim of the springform pan and cut into 8 slices.

6. Store leftover cake in a sealed container or gallon-sized zip-top plastic bag for up to a week.

CALORIES: 296   FAT: 26.4g   PROTEIN: 7.4g   CARBS: 8.4g   FIBER: 5.8g   SUGAR ALCOHOL: 24g

PROTEIN CAKE WITH BUTTERCREAM FROSTING

MAKES: 8 servings   **PREP TIME:** 20 minutes   **COOK TIME:** 30 minutes

This is without a doubt the dessert we make more often than any other. It's truly a guilt-free treat. The carbs are super low, and it tastes great! We often omit the frosting and have it in the morning with a big cup of coffee.

CAKE:

2¾ ounces cream cheese (⅓ cup), room temperature

¼ cup (½ stick) unsalted butter, melted

2 large eggs, room temperature

¼ cup sour cream

10 drops of liquid stevia

1 teaspoon vanilla extract

2 scoops flavored whey protein powder of choice (see Note)

¼ cup oat fiber

1½ teaspoons baking powder

½ teaspoon cream of tartar

VANILLA BUTTERCREAM FROSTING:
(makes 2½ cups)

1 cup (2 sticks) unsalted butter, room temperature

1½ cups powdered erythritol

2 tablespoons heavy whipping cream

1 teaspoon vanilla extract

1. Preheat the oven to 325°F and grease an 8 by 4-inch loaf pan with coconut oil spray.

2. Make the cake: In a large bowl, using a hand mixer, beat the cream cheese and butter until creamy. Add the eggs, sour cream, stevia, and vanilla extract and mix to combine. Set aside.

3. In a small bowl, whisk together the protein powder, oat fiber, baking powder, and cream of tartar. In 2 batches, add the dry mixture to the wet mixture and combine using the mixer until you have a pourable batter.

4. Pour the batter into the greased loaf pan and bake for 30 minutes, until golden brown. Allow the cake to cool completely in the pan before removing and frosting.

5. Make the frosting: Put the butter and erythritol in a medium-sized mixing bowl and beat using the hand mixer or a whisk until light and creamy. Add the cream and vanilla extract and whisk again to combine. Store in the refrigerator until ready to use.

6. Assemble the cake: Remove the cooled cake from the pan and, with the knife held parallel to the top, slice it in half horizontally to create two thin rectangular layers. Cut each layer into 8 equal-sized pieces to create a total of 16 pieces. Using half of the frosting, frost the top of each piece of cake, then stack the layers, two per stack, to make 8 mini two-layer protein cakes.

7. Store leftover cake in a sealed container in the refrigerator for up to a week and leftover frosting in a sealed container in the refrigerator for up to 2 weeks.

CALORIES: 250   FAT: 23.4g   PROTEIN: 8.8g   CARBS: 3.3g   FIBER: 2.5g   SUGAR ALCOHOL: 18g

CHEWY CHOCOLATE CHIP COOKIES

MAKES: 16 cookies (1 per serving)   **PREP TIME:** 10 minutes   **COOK TIME:** 20 minutes

It took us a long time to get this recipe right. We must have gone through 20 or 30 test runs before we learned about the secret ingredient: beef gelatin powder. Our friend Deana, the owner of Good Dee's low-carb baking mixes, tipped us off to the magic of beef gelatin powder, and it took our cookies to the next level.

1½ cups blanched almond flour

½ cup granular erythritol

1 tablespoon unflavored beef gelatin powder

1 teaspoon baking powder

½ cup (1 stick) unsalted butter, melted but not hot

1 large egg

1 teaspoon vanilla extract

½ cup sugar-free chocolate chips

1. Preheat the oven to 350°F and line 2 baking sheets with parchment paper.

2. Put the almond flour, erythritol, gelatin, and baking powder in a medium-sized bowl and whisk using a fork. Set aside.

3. Put the melted butter, egg, and vanilla extract in a large bowl and combine using a hand mixer or whisk. Add the dry mixture to wet mixture in 2 batches and combine until you have a soft dough that can easily be rolled between your hands without sticking.

4. Fold the chocolate chips into the dough with a rubber spatula. Using a cookie scoop or spoon, scoop 16 even-sized balls of the dough onto the baking sheets, leaving 2 inches of space between them. Using your hand or the spatula, flatten the cookies a little. They will spread slightly in the oven.

5. Bake for 20 minutes, or until golden brown. Allow to cool on the baking sheets for 15 minutes prior to handling.

6. Store leftovers in a sealed container in the refrigerator for up to a week or freeze for up to a month.

CALORIES: 125   FAT: 11.8g   PROTEIN: 2.8g   CARBS: 3.2g   FIBER: 1.5g   SUGAR ALCOHOL: 6.6g

BLACKBERRY MINI CHEESECAKES

MAKES: two 4-inch cheesecakes (8 servings)   **ACTIVE PREP TIME:** 10 minutes
INACTIVE PREP TIME: 3 hours   **COOK TIME:** 13 minutes

We use fruit sparingly in our cooking, but when we do use it, we usually go with blackberries. Blackberries have a great flavor and are one of the lowest-carb fruits. We love the pairing of blackberries and the walnut crust in this recipe, pulled together by a soft cheesecake filling.

CRUST:

2½ ounces raw walnuts

3 tablespoons unsalted butter

1 large egg yolk

¼ teaspoon plus 10 drops of liquid stevia

¼ teaspoon pink Himalayan salt

FILLING:

12 ounces cream cheese (1½ cups), room temperature

¼ cup plus 2 tablespoons sour cream

¾ cup heavy whipping cream

¾ cup powdered erythritol

3½ ounces fresh blackberries (about ¾ cup), halved, plus extra whole berries for garnish

NOTE

You can swap in any berry you want in this recipe; however, note that the nutritional information will change.

1. Make the crust: Put all the crust ingredients in a food processor and process until finely chopped and fully combined. Divide the crust mixture between two 4-inch springform pans. Using a rubber spatula, flatten the crusts to cover the bottoms of the pans. Place in the freezer to chill for 30 minutes.

2. Preheat the oven to 325°F. Bake the chilled crusts for 13 minutes, or until slightly browned. Allow to cool completely before adding the filling.

3. Make the filling: Put the cream cheese, sour cream, and heavy cream in a large mixing bowl and combine using a hand mixer until the mixture has a thick, creamy consistency. Add the erythritol and mix to combine.

4. Fold in the halved blackberries. Pour the filling over the cooled crusts and use a rubber spatula to spread the filling evenly.

5. Freeze for at least 2½ hours or refrigerate for at least 6 hours prior to unmolding and serving. If you freeze the cheesecakes, allow them to sit out at room temperature for 10 minutes prior to serving. Garnish each cake with a few blackberries. To serve, cut each cheesecake into quarters, yielding a total of 8 servings.

6. Store leftovers in a sealed container in the refrigerator for up to a week.

CALORIES: 482   FAT: 48.5g   PROTEIN: 7.5g   CARBS: 7.3g   FIBER: 1.7g   SUGAR ALCOHOL: 24g

EXTREME FUDGE BROWNIES

MAKES: 9 brownies (1 per serving) **PREP TIME:** 10 minutes **COOK TIME:** 52 minutes

Let's face it: everyone is a fudgy brownie person, even your weird friend who says he likes cake brownies better. You know deep down even that guy is on team fudge. These are without a doubt the fudgiest keto brownies in existence, and this is the number-one dessert recipe on our blog.

¼ cup cocoa powder

2 tablespoons coconut flour

¼ teaspoon pink Himalayan salt

3 large eggs

½ cup granular erythritol

½ teaspoon vanilla extract

¾ cup (1½ sticks) unsalted butter

2 ounces unsweetened baking chocolate (100% cacao)

Powdered erythritol, for topping (optional)

TWIST

Megha likes to swirl a mixture of softened cream cheese and powdered erythritol into the top of the brownies prior to baking for a simple take on cheesecake brownies!

1. Preheat the oven to 325°F and grease an 8-inch square brownie pan with coconut oil spray.

2. Put the cocoa powder, coconut flour, and salt in a small bowl and whisk using a fork. Set aside.

3. In a large bowl, whisk together the eggs, erythritol, and vanilla extract. Set aside.

4. In a small microwave-safe bowl, combine the butter and chocolate. Microwave until fully melted, about 1 minute, stirring every 30 seconds. Add the melted chocolate mixture to the egg mixture and whisk to combine.

5. Add the dry mixture to the wet mixture in 2 batches, whisking after each addition until fully combined.

6. Pour the batter into the greased pan and bake for 50 minutes, or until a toothpick inserted in the center comes out clean. Allow to cool in the pan for 20 minutes, then cut into 9 pieces. If desired, dust with powdered erythritol before serving.

7. Store leftovers in a sealed container in the refrigerator for up to a week or freeze for up to a month.

CALORIES: 210 FAT: 19.9g PROTEIN: 3.7g CARBS: 4.1g FIBER: 2.8g SUGAR ALCOHOL: 10.7g

COCONUT CHOCOLATE COOKIES

MAKES: 1 dozen cookies (1 per serving)   **PREP TIME:** 10 minutes   **COOK TIME:** 15 minutes

We share a love for anything that combines chocolate and coconut. Not only do these flavors pair perfectly, but they are a natural fit for ketogenic baking. Coconut flour and cocoa powder are naturally low in carbs and, when combined in the right ratio, make for a chewy cookie that the whole family will love.

¼ cup (½ stick) unsalted butter, room temperature

1 ounce cream cheese (2 tablespoons), room temperature

¼ cup plus 2 tablespoons powdered erythritol

1 large egg

¼ cup heavy whipping cream

¼ cup coconut flour

¼ cup cocoa powder

½ teaspoon baking powder

¼ teaspoon pink Himalayan salt

½ cup unsweetened coconut flakes

1. Preheat the oven to 325°F and line 2 baking sheets with parchment paper.

2. In a large bowl, use a hand mixer to cream the butter, cream cheese, and erythritol until light and fluffy. Mix in the egg and cream. Set aside.

3. In a small bowl, whisk together the coconut flour, cocoa powder, baking powder, and salt. Add the dry mixture to the wet ingredients in 2 batches, mixing with the hand mixer after each addition until you achieve a soft, slightly crumbly consistency. Fold in the coconut flakes.

4. Using a cookie scoop or spoon, scoop 12 even-sized balls of the dough onto the lined baking sheets and flatten with a fork to the desired size. They will not spread in the oven. Bake for 15 minutes, or until slightly firm to touch. Allow to cool on the baking sheets for 20 minutes prior to handling or they will fall apart.

5. Store in a sealed container or zip-top plastic bag in the refrigerator for up to a week.

TWIST

Matt likes to add chopped pecans and chocolate chips for a simple take on kitchen sink cookies!

CALORIES: 91   FAT: 8.4g   PROTEIN: 1.4g   CARBS: 3g   FIBER: 1.8g   SUGAR ALCOHOL: 5g

PEANUT BUTTER HEMP HEART COOKIES

MAKES: 1 dozen cookies (1 per serving)   **PREP TIME:** 10 minutes   **COOK TIME:** 14 minutes

Hemp hearts are one of our favorite ingredients to work with. They are high in fiber, protein, and fat and have a nice earthy taste. Hemp hearts give these cookies a rich flavor and boost the nutrient content.

½ cup natural peanut butter, room temperature

1 large egg

½ cup hemp hearts

¼ cup granular erythritol

¼ teaspoon baking powder

½ teaspoon vanilla extract

½ cup sugar-free chocolate chips

1. Preheat the oven to 350°F and line 2 baking sheets with parchment paper.

2. In a large mixing bowl, combine the peanut butter and egg using a whisk. Add the hemp hearts, erythritol, baking powder, and vanilla extract and combine using a wooden spoon. Fold in the chocolate chips.

3. Using a cookie scoop or spoon, scoop 12 even-sized balls of the dough onto the lined baking sheets, spacing them about 2 inches apart. Flatten the cookies with a fork.

4. Bake the cookies for 12 to 14 minutes, until golden brown and slightly firm to touch. Allow to cool on the baking sheets for 10 minutes prior to handling or they will fall apart.

5. Store leftovers in a sealed container in the refrigerator for up to a week or freeze for up to a month.

CALORIES: 120   FAT: 9.8g   PROTEIN: 5.7g   CARBS: 4.1g   FIBER: 2.2g   SUGAR ALCOHOL: 4.8g

COUNTY FAIR CINNAMON DONUTS

MAKES: 6 donuts (1 per serving) **PREP TIME:** 10 minutes **COOK TIME:** 25 minutes

The county fair has some of the best-tasting food we've ever tried. We don't even remember anything else about the fair. We went with the sole focus of consuming as much fried delicacies as humanly possible. These baked donuts have the same cinnamon-sugar flavor that will take you back to your childhood fair days!

11½ ounces cream cheese (1 cup plus 7 tablespoons), room temperature

½ cup extra-virgin olive oil

¼ cup heavy whipping cream

4 large eggs

½ teaspoon liquid stevia

½ teaspoon maple extract

½ teaspoon vanilla extract

¼ cup plus 2 tablespoons coconut flour

2 teaspoons ground cinnamon

1 teaspoon baking powder

1 teaspoon xanthan gum

¼ teaspoon pink Himalayan salt

TOPPING:

¼ cup granular erythritol

¼ cup ground cinnamon

Special equipment:

6-cavity silicone donut pan

1. Preheat the oven to 400°F and grease a 6-cavity donut pan with coconut oil spray.

2. In a large bowl, beat the cream cheese, olive oil, cream, eggs, stevia, and extracts using a hand mixer until smooth and fully incorporated. Set aside.

3. In a small bowl, whisk together the coconut flour, cinnamon, baking powder, xanthan gum, and salt using a whisk. Add the dry mixture to the wet ingredients and combine using the hand mixer. Fill the greased cavities of the donut mold to the brim, making sure not to overfill.

4. Bake for 25 minutes, until the donuts are puffed up and a toothpick comes out clean.

5. Meanwhile, put the ingredients for the topping on a plate and combine using your fingers. After removing the donuts from the oven, allow to cool in the pan for 5 minutes, then toss them, one at a time, in the cinnamon-sugar mixture. Set the coated donuts on a wire baking rack to cool for an additional 10 minutes prior to eating.

6. Store leftovers in a sealed container in the refrigerator for up to 4 days.

CALORIES: 461 FAT: 44.8g PROTEIN: 8.7g CARBS: 6.8g FIBER: 2.5g SUGARALCOHOL: 8g

PISTACHIO COCONUT FUDGE

MAKES: 16 pieces (1 piece per serving)   **ACTIVE PREP TIME:** 10 minutes
INACTIVE PREP TIME: 2 hours

When Matt was a child, his family took plenty of trips to Mackinac Island, Michigan, the fudge capital of the world. They would ride bikes around the island fueled entirely by fudge. His favorite was the pistachio fudge, which was the inspiration for this recipe.

½ cup coconut oil, melted

4 ounces cream cheese (½ cup), room temperature

1 teaspoon vanilla extract

¼ teaspoon plus 10 drops of liquid stevia

½ cup shelled raw pistachios, roughly chopped, divided

½ cup unsweetened shredded coconut, divided

1. In a medium-sized bowl, beat the coconut oil and cream cheese with a hand mixer until smooth and creamy. Add the vanilla extract and stevia and mix until combined.

2. Fold in one-third of the pistachios and one-third of the coconut flakes using a rubber spatula. Pour the fudge mixture into a 5-inch square dish or pan and top with the remaining pistachios and shredded coconut.

3. Refrigerate for at least 2 hours prior to serving. To serve, cut into 16 pieces.

4. Store leftovers in a sealed container in the refrigerator for up to a week.

CALORIES: 123   FAT: 12.9g   PROTEIN: 1.2g   CARBS 2g   FIBER: 0.7g

STRAWBERRY SHORTCAKES

MAKES: 6 servings **PREP TIME:** 20 minutes **COOK TIME:** 20 minutes

Keto desserts tend to be dense and heavy. These fluffy strawberry shortcakes are the complete opposite. Piled high with homemade whipped cream and fresh strawberries, they are the perfect summer treat.

SHORTCAKES:

¼ cup plus 2 tablespoons coconut flour

1 packet sugar-free strawberry-flavored gelatin powder

1 teaspoon baking powder

¼ teaspoon pink Himalayan salt

¼ cup plus 2 tablespoons coconut oil, melted

2 ounces cream cheese (¼ cup), room temperature

¼ cup sour cream

4 large eggs, room temperature

15 drops of liquid stevia

FILLING/TOPPING:

1 cup heavy whipping cream

1 cup fresh strawberries, hulled and thinly sliced

Special equipment:

6-cavity, 3½-inch-diameter silicone muffin top pan

1. Preheat the oven to 350°F and grease a 6-cavity silicone muffin top pan with coconut oil spray.

2. Make the shortcakes: In a small bowl, whisk together the coconut flour, gelatin, baking powder, and salt.

3. Put the coconut oil, cream cheese, and sour cream in a large mixing bowl and combine with the whisk. Add the eggs and stevia and whisk until smooth.

4. Add the dry mixture to the wet ingredients and whisk until fully incorporated and smooth. Evenly distribute the mixture among the greased cavities of the muffin top pan, filling them to the rim. Level the tops with a butter knife.

5. Bake for 20 minutes, or until a toothpick inserted in the center of a cake comes out clean. Allow to cool in the pan for 5 minutes, then transfer the shortcakes to a cooling rack to cool completely before filling.

6. Make the filling/topping: Put the cream in a medium-sized mixing bowl and beat using a hand mixer until stiff peaks form.

7. Assemble the shortcakes: Slice the cakes in half horizontally to create a total of 12 round layers. Using a butter knife, frost the bottom halves with the whipped cream, then make a single layer of overlapping strawberries. Put the other half of each cake on top of the strawberries and frost the tops using a piping bag or butter knife. Make a top layer of sliced strawberries. (We like to fan the berry slices for a pretty presentation.)

8. Store leftovers in a sealed container in the refrigerator for up to a week.

CALORIES: 392   FAT: 36.8g   PROTEIN: 6.2g   CARBS: 8.6g   FIBER: 3g

VANILLA EGG CUSTARD

MAKES: 2 servings   **ACTIVE PREP TIME:** 10 minutes   **INACTIVE PREP TIME:** 2 hours
COOK TIME: 30 minutes

This delicate egg custard is the perfect date-night dessert because it looks and tastes fancy but is absolutely foolproof.

1 cup heavy whipping cream, plus ¼ cup for topping if desired

2 large egg yolks

2 teaspoons vanilla extract

½ teaspoon liquid stevia

1. Preheat the oven to 300°F.

2. Put the 1 cup of cream, egg yolks, vanilla extract, and stevia in a medium-sized mixing bowl and beat with a hand mixer until combined. Pour into two 6-ounce ramekins. Place the ramekins in a baking dish and fill the baking dish with boiling water so that it goes two-thirds of the way up the sides of the ramekins.

3. Bake for 30 minutes, or until the edges of the custard are just starting to brown. It should not be completely baked through and firm. Place in the refrigerator to chill and set for at least 2 hours before serving.

4. If making the topping, put the ¼ cup of cream in a medium-sized mixing bowl and whip using the hand mixer until soft peaks form. Top the custard with the whipped cream prior to serving.

TWIST

After the custard has chilled, Megha likes to break through the top and swirl in some chocolate chips and pumpkin pie spice for greater richness and a fall spin!

CALORIES: 568   FAT: 59.5g   PROTEIN: 5.5g   CARBS: 4.5g   FIBER: 0g

INSTANT PROTEIN ICE CREAM

MAKES: 1 serving   **PREP TIME:** 1 minute

Dessert doesn't have to be complex or require five different mixing bowls, especially on those busy days when you barely have enough energy to cook dinner. You can make this delicious low-carb protein ice cream in under two minutes.

1 cup unsweetened almond milk

1 scoop flavored protein powder of choice

¼ teaspoon xanthan gum

1½ cups ice

Ground cinnamon, for garnish (optional)

1. Put the milk in a blender. Add the protein powder, xanthan gum, and ice and puree on high until the mixture is smooth, 20 to 30 seconds.

2. Pour into a serving bowl and garnish with a dusting of cinnamon, if desired. Enjoy immediately.

NOTES

We use cinnamon crunch–flavored Quest Protein Powder, but any powder you have at home will work!

You can up the fat by adding some heavy whipping cream or MCT oil.

CALORIES: 130   FAT: 5g   PROTEIN: 21g   CARBS: 5g   FIBER: 2g

—Chapter 8—

CONDIMENTS

PEANUT SAUCE

MAKES: ¾ cup (2 tablespoons per serving)   **PREP TIME:** 5 minutes

This is the go-to sauce in our household for a couple reasons. The first is that it contains peanut butter, which is pretty much the perfect food. The second is that it is so easy to make. All it takes is a handful of ingredients, a blender, and five minutes. This sauce pairs particularly well with Asian dishes.

½ cup natural peanut butter

2 cloves garlic

1 (½-inch) piece fresh ginger, grated

¼ cup water

2 tablespoons soy sauce

1 tablespoon unseasoned rice wine vinegar

10 drops of liquid stevia

½ teaspoon red pepper flakes

FOR GARNISH (OPTIONAL):

Chopped raw peanuts

Sliced scallions

1. Put all the ingredients for the sauce in a blender or food processor and process until smooth. Check the consistency and add more water to thin the sauce, if desired.

2. Pour the sauce into a bowl and garnish with chopped peanuts and sliced scallions, if desired.

3. Store in a sealed container in the refrigerator for up to a week.

TIP

If you don't have rice wine vinegar, you can substitute an equal amount of lime juice.

CALORIES: 134   FAT: 10.7g   PROTEIN: 6.3g   CARBS: 5.8g   FIBER: 2g

BBQ SAUCE

MAKES: 1¾ cups plus 2 tablespoons (5 tablespoons per serving)
PREP TIME: 5 minutes **COOK TIME:** 25 minutes

This tangy apple-flavored barbecue sauce will steal the show at your next cookout. We usually make a big batch and store it in a mason jar in the fridge.

1 cup reduced-sugar ketchup

½ cup water

¼ cup apple cider vinegar

2½ tablespoons sugar-free maple syrup

2 teaspoons ground black pepper

1 teaspoon Worcestershire sauce

½ teaspoon liquid smoke

½ teaspoon onion powder

¼ teaspoon pink Himalayan salt

1. Put all the ingredients in a small saucepan and combine using a whisk. Bring to a boil over high heat, then reduce the heat and simmer for 15 to 20 minutes, until the desired consistency is achieved. The longer you reduce the sauce on the stovetop, the thicker it will get and the more concentrated the flavors will become.

2. Store in a sealed container in the refrigerator for up to 2 weeks.

CALORIES: 17 FAT: 0g PROTEIN: 0g CARBS: 3.5g FIBER: 0.3g SUGAR ALCOHOL: 0.3g

HOMEMADE CHIPOTLE MAYO

MAKES: 1¾ cups plus 2 tablespoons (1 tablespoon per serving)   **PREP TIME:** 5 minutes

Store-bought mayo is usually made with vegetable oils that are loaded with harmful trans fats. This is a healthy alternative you can feel good about piling onto your next sandwich. We use avocado oil and spice it up with some ground chipotle pepper for a little kick. To make a plain mayo, simply omit the chipotle pepper (see the variation below)—or do what we often do and pick up a jar of Primal Kitchen's ready-made avocado oil mayo.

2 large egg yolks

2 tablespoons Dijon mustard

1 tablespoon apple cider vinegar

1 teaspoon ground chipotle pepper

½ teaspoon pink Himalayan salt

1½ cups avocado oil

1. Put the egg yolks, mustard, vinegar, chipotle pepper, and salt in a food processor and pulse to combine.

2. With the processor running, *very* slowly pour in the oil until you use it all and the mayo becomes thick.

3. Store in a sealed container in the refrigerator for up to 2 weeks.

NOTES

It should take you 3 to 4 minutes to drizzle in the oil to achieve the proper consistency!

This recipe calls for consuming raw eggs, which we are comfortable doing. If you are concerned, feel free to use pasteurized eggs.

VARIATION

HOMEMADE MAYO. To make a plain, unflavored mayo, simply omit the ground chipotle pepper.

CALORIES: 101   FAT: 11.5g   PROTEIN: 0.1g   CARBS: 0.1g   FIBER: 0g

MAPLE CINNAMON ALMOND BUTTER

MAKES: 1¼ cups (2 tablespoons per serving)   **PREP TIME:** 5 minutes
COOK TIME: 20 minutes

What could possibly be better than almond butter? How about roasted maple cinnamon almond butter? We make different types of nut butter at home all the time, and this is by far the best version we've made. We like to spread it on slices of our homemade keto bread (page 76) or on pancakes (page 60)—or just eat it by the spoonful!

2 cups raw almonds

2 tablespoons coconut oil, melted

1½ teaspoons ground cinnamon

¾ teaspoon maple extract

¼ teaspoon plus 5 drops of liquid stevia

1. Preheat the oven to 300°F.

2. Pour the almonds onto a rimmed baking sheet and drizzle with the coconut oil. Using your hands or a spoon, toss to coat the almonds.

3. Roast for 20 minutes, until the almonds are dried out and feel lighter in weight. Remove from the oven and allow to cool.

4. Transfer the cooled almonds to a food processor and process for 1 minute, until you have a thick, ground meal. Add the cinnamon, maple extract, and stevia and process for an additional 3 minutes, until smooth and creamy.

5. Store in a sealed container in the refrigerator for up to 2 weeks.

NOTE

The processing time may vary depending on the speed and power of your food processor.

TWIST

Megha has a tree nut allergy, so she swaps out the almonds for peanuts in this recipe. Give it a try!

CALORIES: 190   FAT: 17.1g   PROTEIN: 6g   CARBS: 6.5g   FIBER: 3.8g

STRAWBERRY CHIA SEED JAM

MAKES: roughly 1½ cups (1¼ tablespoons per serving) **PREP TIME:** 15 minutes
COOK TIME: 20 minutes

We love taking advantage of the natural thickening ability of chia seeds in a variety of recipes. This strawberry jam is just one example. Peanut butter and jelly sandwiches are back on the menu!

1 pound fresh strawberries, hulled and halved

½ cup water

½ teaspoon plus 10 drops of liquid stevia

¼ cup chia seeds

1. Bring the strawberries and water to a boil in a heavy-bottomed saucepan over medium-high heat.

2. Once boiling, use a spoon to smash the strawberries in the saucepan. Add the stevia, reduce the heat to a simmer, and cook for an additional 10 to 15 minutes, until the mixture has a thick, jamlike consistency.

3. Turn off the heat, add the chia seeds, and stir for 1 to 2 minutes.

4. Store in a sealed container in the refrigerator for up to 3 months.

TIP

You can swap out the strawberries for any other berry, but be aware that doing so will change the nutritional information of this recipe.

CALORIES: 24   FAT: 0.8g   PROTEIN: 0.9g   CARBS: 3.4g   FIBER: 1.8g

Keto Meal Plans

In this section, there are six different one-week meal plans that showcase varying eating styles:

- **Tony** finds that eating two meals a day suits his busy schedule and his disdain for cooking.

- **Sally** likes having something sweet every day.

- **Brenda** sticks to the basics and eats whole foods.

- **Marty** is a vegetarian and still makes a ketogenic diet work for him.

- **Matt** likes to keep carbs very low and fat high in two large daily meals.

- **Megha** likes variety, lots of veggies, and snacks.

Rather than try to create basic meal plans that are one-size-fits-all, we thought that providing a week of different ways of eating a ketogenic diet would be of more value. Take pieces of each of these plans to create a way of eating that you find fulfilling and sustainable.

Although these plans can be followed to a T, they are best used as references for inspiration and as a visual aid to what a keto diet looks like. As you can see, no two people's keto diets are the same. It's important to find what works for you. Add more of the foods you enjoy and take out the foods you don't.

Note: Unless otherwise specified, the plans assume that you will eat one serving of each dish as defined in the recipe. The nutritional information that we have provided for each plan is based on these portion sizes.

MEAL PLAN 1:
TWO-MEAL TONY

When eating keto, most people find it advantageous and natural to break out of the conventional three-meals-a-day paradigm. Switching to two larger meals per day can be beneficial and easier to maintain for several reasons. First, hunger is different on keto. You will no longer be a prisoner to carb cravings and the blood sugar roller coaster, so it will be easier to go longer between meals and be productive without having to eat every few hours. Another good reason is that most keto meals need to be prepared. Cooking three meals a day can be time-consuming and could make the diet unsustainable. Switching to bigger, less frequent meals is a good way to counter that and seems to be more in tune with the way human beings have eaten throughout history. It's important to note, though, that a decrease in number of meals does not mean a decrease in number of calories consumed. You're still eating the same amount of food, just condensed into fewer meals.

We like to add stevia and vanilla extract to our butter coffees.

Fat bombs are an easy way to add fat to a meal.

			CALORIES	FAT	PROTEIN	CARBS	NET CARBS
DAY 1	7:00 AM	Black coffee	0	0g	0g	0g	0g
	10:00 AM	Butter coffee (Blend 1 tablespoon butter into brewed coffee.)	100	11g	0g	0g	0g
		2 servings *Three-Cheese Spinach Frittata*	296	21g	21g	3g	3g
	NOON	1 avocado	235	20g	3g	12g	2g
		2 servings *Pistachio Coconut Fudge*	245	26g	2.5g	4g	2.5g
	6:00 PM	2 servings *Crispy Chicken Thighs with Pan Sauce*	620	42g	71g	6.5g	6g
	8:00 PM	Tea	0	0g	0g	0g	0g
			1496	120g 68.7%	97.5g 24.8%	25.5g 6.5%	13.5g 3.4%

40
Three-Cheese Spinach Frittata

234
Pistachio Coconut Fudge

108
Crispy Chicken Thighs with Pan Sauce

DAY 2

		CALORIES	FAT	PROTEIN	CARBS	NET CARBS
7:00 AM	Butter coffee	100	11g	0g	0g	0g
10:00 AM	Butter coffee	100	11g	0g	0g	0g
	3 hard-boiled eggs	240	15g	18g	1.5g	1.5g
NOON	1 tin sardines packed in olive oil	150	11g	13g	0g	0g
	1 string cheese	80	6g	7g	0g	0g
6:00 PM	2 servings *Mama's Meatloaf*	700	55g	42g	6g	4g
7:00 PM	*Protein Cake with Buttercream Frosting*	170	14g	5g	7g	2.5g
		1540	123g	85g	14.5g	8g
			73.6%	22.6%	3.9%	2.1%

> Hard-boiled eggs, sardines, and string cheese was Megha's typical lunch when she used to work an office job.

Butter coffee is by no means an essential part of a keto diet; it's just something we have grown to love. We rarely go a single day without it.

120
Mama's Meatloaf

220
Protein Cake with Buttercream Frosting

DAY 3

		CALORIES	FAT	PROTEIN	CARBS	NET CARBS
7:00 AM	Butter coffee	100	12g	0g	0g	0g
10:00 AM	Black coffee	0	0g	0g	0g	0g
	2 slices *The Best Keto Bread*	225	20g	9g	5g	3g
NOON	2 tablespoons butter	200	22g	0g	0g	0g
	4 prosciutto and mozzarella roll-ups	240	15g	28g	1g	1g
	10 ounces rib-eye steak	675	52.5g	47.5g	0g	0g
6:00 PM	2 cups broccoli	60	0g	2g	8g	4g
	1 tablespoon butter	100	11g	0g	0g	0g
8:00 PM	Tea	0	0g	0g	0g	0g
		1600	132.5g	86.5g	14g	8g
			74.8%	21.7%	3.5%	2%

> Use ½ ounce each of prosciutto and mozzarella per roll-up.

> Keto bread is great for packing in your work lunch.

76
The Best Keto Bread

DAY 4

		CALORIES	FAT	PROTEIN	CARBS	NET CARBS
7:00 AM	Butter coffee	100	11g	0g	0g	0g
10:00 AM	Butter coffee	100	11g	0g	0g	0g
NOON	2 *California Collard Wraps*	700	46g	50g	20g	6g
	2 servings *Pistachio Coconut Fudge*	245	26g	2.5g	4g	2.5g
6:00 PM	2 servings *Crispy Chicken Thighs with Pan Sauce*	620	42g	71g	6.5g	6g
8:00 PM	Tea	0	0g	0g	0g	0g
		1765	136g	123.5g	30.5g	14.5g
			66.5%	26.9%	6.6%	3.2%

168
California Collard Wraps

leftover
Pistachio Coconut Fudge

leftover
Crispy Chicken Thighs with Pan Sauce

DAY 5

		CALORIES	FAT	PROTEIN	CARBS	NET CARBS
7:00 AM	Black coffee	0	0g	0g	0g	0g
10:00 AM	Black coffee	0	0g	0g	0g	0g
NOON	2 servings *Three-Cheese Spinach Frittata*	296	21g	21g	3g	3g
	1 avocado	235	20g	3g	12g	2g
	2 servings *Sweet and Spicy Beef Jerky*	300	19.5g	31.5g	1g	1g
	Chipotle Dry-Rub Wings	507	36g	42.5g	3g	3g
6:00 PM	Celery	15	0g	0g	4g	2g
	Blue cheese dressing	130	13g	1g	1g	0g
7:00 PM	2 *Chewy Chocolate Chip Cookies*	250	24g	5.5g	6.5g	3.5g
		1733	133.5g	104.5g	30.5g	14.5g
			69%	24%	7%	3.3%

> Frittatas are highly customizable and are even better reheated the next couple days after they are made.

leftover

Three-Cheese Spinach Frittata

186

Sweet and Spicy Beef Jerky

142

Chipotle Dry-Rub Wings

222

Chewy Chocolate Chip Cookies

> You have to try these cookies!

DAY 6

		CALORIES	FAT	PROTEIN	CARBS	NET CARBS
7:00 AM	Butter coffee	100	11g	0g	0g	0g
10:00 AM	Black coffee	0	0g	0g	0g	0g
	Overnight Protein Oats	439	28g	39g	9g	1g
NOON	1 string cheese	80	6g	7g	0g	0g
	½ ounce macadamia nuts	100	10g	1g	2g	1g
6:00 PM	1 *Double Bacon Cheeseburger*	820	60g	65g	6g	5g
	Side salad (2 cups spinach with salt, pepper, and 1 tablespoon olive oil)	130	14g	2g	2g	1g
8:00 PM	Tea	0	0g	0g	0g	0g
		1669	129g	114g	19g	8g
			68.6%	26.9%	4.5%	1.9%

> We make a big batch of overnight oats for grab-and-go breakfasts during busy weeks.

50

Overnight Protein Oats

126

Double Bacon Cheeseburger

DAY 7

		CALORIES	FAT	PROTEIN	CARBS	NET CARBS
7:00 AM	Butter coffee	100	11g	0g	0g	0g
10:00 AM	Black coffee	0	0g	0g	0g	0g
	Microwave Bread	285	25g	10g	6g	2g
NOON	2 slices bacon	90	7g	5g	0g	0g
	2 eggs	160	10g	12g	1g	1g
6:00 PM	1 ounce cheddar cheese	110	9g	7g	0g	0g
	2 servings *Spicy Shrimp Fried Rice*	566	26.5g	63.5g	25.5g	17.5g
7:00 PM	*Snickerdoodle Cream Cheesecake*	403	36g	11g	12g	4g
8:00 PM	Tea	0	0g	0g	0g	0g
		1714	124.5g	108.5g	44.5g	24.5g
			64.7%	25.1%	10.3%	5.7%

> You haven't lived until you've tried a breakfast sandwich on Microwave Bread. It tastes so much better than it sounds!

74

Microwave Bread

134

Spicy Shrimp Fried Rice

214

Snickerdoodle Cream Cheesecake

> Microwaved mug cakes are our favorite quick after-dinner desserts.

SALLY SWEET TOOTH

This is the dessert-every-night meal plan. Like us, we're sure lots of you out there have a sweet tooth. Some are born with it, and others develop it over years of eating a standard American diet. Whatever the case may be, there are some good alternatives that you can rely on when starting a keto diet! While desserts are best used as occasional treats, you must do anything you can to get yourself off the "real" desserts. Keto desserts are great transition foods as you begin your healthy-eating journey.

DAY 1

			CALORIES	FAT	PROTEIN	CARBS	NET CARBS
7:00 AM	Coffee with heavy cream and stevia (2 tablespoons heavy cream)		100	10g	0g	0g	0g
8:30 AM	*Golden Gate Granola*		200	18g	5g	5.5g	2g
NOON	3 servings *Three-Cheese Spinach Frittata*		444	31.5g	31.5g	4.5g	4.5g
	1 avocado		235	20g	3g	12g	2g
6:00 PM	*Crispy Chicken Thighs with Pan Sauce*		308	21g	35.5g	3.5g	3g
	1 *Extreme Fudge Brownie*		210	20g	3.5g	4g	1.5g
8:00 PM	Tea with heavy cream and stevia		100	10g	0g	0g	0g
			1597	130.5g	78.5g	29.5g	13g
				73.1%	19.6%	7.4%	3.2%

> Make a big batch and have it ready for the week!

> The ultimate dessert for crushing chocolate cravings!

Golden Gate Granola — 56

Three-Cheese Spinach Frittata — 40

Crispy Chicken Thighs with Pan Sauce — 108

Extreme Fudge Brownies — 226

DAY 2

			CALORIES	FAT	PROTEIN	CARBS	NET CARBS
7:00 AM	Coffee with heavy cream and stevia (2 tablespoons heavy cream)		100	10g	0g	0g	0g
8:30 AM	½ ounce macadamia nuts		100	10g	1g	2g	1g
	2 hard-boiled eggs		160	10g	12g	1g	1g
	1 *Raspberry Fiber Muffin*		131	10.5g	4g	11g	1g
NOON	1 tablespoon butter		100	10g	0g	0g	0g
	Chipotle Dry-Rub Wings		507	36g	42.5g	3g	3g
6:00 PM	6 ounces rib-eye steak with butter		405	31.5g	28.5g	0g	0g
	Asparagus with Goat Cheese and Sunflower Seeds		148	10g	7.5g	6.5g	4g
7:00 PM	2 *Peanut Butter Hemp Heart Cookies*		240	19.5g	11.5g	8g	3.5g
			1891	147.5g	107g	31.5g	13.5g
				70.6%	22.8%	6.7%	2.9%

> We usually opt for rib-eye and New York strip steaks due to their higher fat content.

Raspberry Fiber Muffins — 78

Chipotle Dry-Rub Wings — 142

Asparagus with Goat Cheese and Sunflower Seeds — 200

Peanut Butter Hemp Heart Cookies — 230

Megha *and* Matt
BAROT GAEDKE

DAY 3

Time	Item	CALORIES	FAT	PROTEIN	CARBS	NET CARBS
7:00 AM	Coffee with heavy cream and stevia (2 tablespoons heavy cream)	100	10g	0g	0g	0g
8:30 AM	*Golden Gate Granola*	200	18g	5g	5.5g	2g
	2 hard-boiled eggs	160	10g	12g	1g	1g
	1 *Raspberry Fiber Muffin*	131	10.5g	4g	11g	1g
NOON	1 tablespoon butter	100	10g	0g	0g	0g
	2 string cheeses	160	12g	14g	0g	0g
	1 serving *Chicken Tenders*	305	16g	38g	3.5g	2.5g
6:00 PM	Blue cheese dressing	130	13g	1g	1g	1g
	2 cups steamed broccoli	60	0g	2g	8g	4g
	1 tablespoon butter	100	11g	0g	0g	0g
7:00 PM	1 *Chewy Chocolate Chip Cookie*	125	12g	3g	3g	1.5g
		1571	122.5g	79g	33g	13g
			71.1%	20.4%	8.5%	3.4%

> We always have hard-boiled eggs in the fridge in case we get hungry between meals.

leftover — *Golden Gate Granola* | *leftover* — *Raspberry Fiber Muffins* | 106 — *Chicken Tenders* | 222 — *Chewy Chocolate Chip Cookies*

DAY 4

Time	Item	CALORIES	FAT	PROTEIN	CARBS	NET CARBS
7:00 AM	Coffee with heavy cream and stevia (2 tablespoons heavy cream)	100	10g	0g	0g	0g
8:30 AM	*Breakfast Roll-ups*	300	23.5g	20.5g	4.5g	3g
	1 tin sardines packed in olive oil	150	11g	13g	0g	0g
NOON	2 slices *The Best Keto Bread*	225	20g	9g	5g	3g
	1 tablespoon butter	100	11g	0g	0g	0g
6:00 PM	*Loaded Cobb Salad*	778	64g	43g	15g	5g
7:00 PM	2 servings *Pistachio Coconut Fudge*	245	26g	2.5g	4g	2.5g
		1898	165.5g	88g	28.5g	13.5g
			76.2%	18%	5.8%	2.8%

> Cobb salads are highly customizable and are easily one of our favorite dinners.

52 — *Breakfast Roll-ups* | 76 — *The Best Keto Bread* | 162 — *Loaded Cobb Salad* | 234 — *Pistachio Coconut Fudge*

DAY 5

Time	Item	CALORIES	FAT	PROTEIN	CARBS	NET CARBS
7:00 AM	Coffee with heavy cream and stevia (2 tablespoons heavy cream)	100	10g	0g	0g	0g
8:30 AM	2 servings *Three-Cheese Spinach Frittata*	296	21g	21g	3g	3g
NOON	*Golden Gate Granola*	200	18g	5g	5.5g	2g
	Mocha Protein Keto Coffee	361	24g	37g	4g	2g
6:00 PM	*Creamy White Chili*	278	18g	24g	3.5g	3g
	Cheddar and Thyme Cornbread	250	21.5g	10.5g	6g	3g
7:00 PM	*Blackberry Mini Cheesecakes*	482	48.5g	7.5g	7.5g	6g
		1967	161g	105g	29.5g	19g
			72.9%	21.1%	5.9%	3.8%

> Chili and cornbread on a low-carb diet?! Yes!

40 — *Three-Cheese Spinach Frittata* | *leftover* — *Golden Gate Granola* | 66 — *Mocha Protein Keto Coffee* | 104 — *Creamy White Chili* | 72 — *Cheddar and Thyme Cornbread* | 224 — *Blackberry Mini Cheesecakes*

		CALORIES	FAT	PROTEIN	CARBS	NET CARBS
7:00 AM	Coffee with heavy cream and stevia (2 tablespoons heavy cream)	100	10g	0g	0g	0g
8:30 AM	*Chocolate Chip Zucchini Bread*	170	13.5g	5g	7g	3g
	1 tablespoon butter	100	10g	0g	0g	0g
NOON	*Curry Chicken Salad*	339	14g	25g	2.5g	1.5g
	1 string cheese	80	6g	7g	0g	0g
6:00 PM	*Beef Satay Skewers*	253	16g	24g	4g	3.5g
	Peanut Sauce	134	10.5g	6.5g	6g	4g
	2 cups steamed broccoli	60	0g	2g	8g	4g
	1 tablespoon butter	100	11g	0g	0g	0g
7:00 PM	*Protein Cake with Buttercream Frosting*	250	23.5g	9g	3.5g	1g
		1586	114.5g	78.5g	31g	17g
			70.2%	21.4%	8.4%	4.6%

Make a big batch of this peanut sauce because it goes with everything...literally everything!

86 *Chocolate Chip Zucchini Bread*

160 *Curry Chicken Salad*

144 *Beef Satay Skewers*

244 *Peanut Sauce*

220 *Protein Cake with Buttercream Frosting*

We often make these protein cakes without the frosting for a dessert we feel good about having more frequently.

		CALORIES	FAT	PROTEIN	CARBS	NET CARBS
7:00 AM	Coffee with heavy cream and stevia (2 tablespoons heavy cream)	100	10g	0g	0g	0g
8:30 AM	2 *Breakfast Cookies*	450	35g	17.5g	24g	9g
NOON	2 servings *Three-Cheese Spinach Frittata*	296	21g	21g	3g	3g
	1 ounce Brazil nuts	210	21g	4g	3g	1g
6:00 PM	2 servings *Caprese Chicken Skillet*	452	23.5g	52.5g	7g	5g
7:00 PM	*Death by Chocolate Cheesecake*	398	37g	7g	11g	5.5g
		1906	147.5g	102g	48g	23.5g
			68.9%	21.2%	10%	4.9%

48 *Breakfast Cookies*

leftover *Three-Cheese Spinach Frittata*

156 *Caprese Chicken Skillet*

210 *Death by Chocolate Cheesecake*

Brazil nuts and macadamia nuts are our top two nut options for a keto diet.

MEAL PLAN 3:
BASIC BRENDA

Keeping it as simple as possible is the best approach to keto. Limiting your diet to whole foods, healthy fats, good sources of protein, and nutrient-rich veggies is a place we all strive to get to at some point. With that being said, it's a process, and going at your own pace is important. Don't feel intimidated if you need to have some keto sweets occasionally to make the diet more sustainable for you. This plan showcases a basic keto diet and some staple meals that are common in our weekly rotation.

DAY 1

		CALORIES	FAT	PROTEIN	CARBS	NET CARBS
7:00 AM	Black coffee	0	0g	0g	0g	0g
	3 eggs	240	15g	18g	1.5g	1.5g
	1 tablespoon butter	100	11g	0g	0g	0g
	4 slices bacon	180	14g	10g	0g	0g
NOON	1 ounce macadamia nuts	200	21g	2g	4g	2g
	Curry Chicken Salad	339	14g	25.5g	2.5g	1.5g
6:00 PM	6 ounces chicken thighs	360	25.5g	30g	0g	0g
	2 cups steamed broccoli	60	0g	2g	8g	4g
	1 tablespoon butter	100	11g	0g	0g	0g
		1579	111.5g	87.5g	16g	9g
			70.8%	24.7%	4.5%	2.5%

> The gold standard keto breakfast.

> You can't go wrong with pan-seared meat, veggies, and some added fat.

160

Curry Chicken Salad

DAY 2

		CALORIES	FAT	PROTEIN	CARBS	NET CARBS
7:00 AM	Black coffee	0	0g	0g	0g	0g
	3 eggs	240	15g	18g	1.5g	1.5g
	1 ounce cheddar cheese	110	9g	7g	0g	0g
	1 tin sardines packed in olive oil	150	11g	13g	0g	0g
NOON	2 slices *The Best Keto Bread*	225	20g	9g	5g	3g
	1 tablespoon butter	100	11g	0g	0g	0g
3:00 PM	1 ounce macadamia nuts	200	21g	2g	4g	2g
6:00 PM	*Loaded Cobb Salad*	778	64g	43g	15g	5g
		1803	151g	92g	25.5g	11.5g
			74.3%	20.1%	5.6%	2.5%

76

The Best Keto Bread

162

Loaded Cobb Salad

DAY 3

> 3 eggs, 4 slices bacon, 1 cup spinach, and 1 ounce cheddar cheese

	CALORIES	FAT	PROTEIN	CARBS	NET CARBS
7:00 AM Black coffee	0	0g	0g	0g	0g
Bacon, spinach, and cheddar omelet	535	40g	36g	2.5g	1.5g
NOON ½ scoop protein powder	60	1g	13g	1g	1g
¼ cup heavy cream	200	20g	0g	1g	1g
1 ounce almonds	180	15g	6g	6g	2g
6:00 PM 6 ounces rib-eye steak	405	31.5g	28.5g	0g	0g
Asparagus with Goat Cheese and Sunflower Seeds	148	10g	7.5g	6.5g	4g
	1528	117.5g	91g	17g	9.5g
		71%	24.4%	4.6%	2.6%

> This is a basic meal replacement recipe. Feel free to upgrade it with some shredded coconut or a handful of berries.

Be sure to cook some extra steak to have for breakfast the next day!

Asparagus with Goat Cheese and Sunflower Seeds

200

DAY 4

	CALORIES	FAT	PROTEIN	CARBS	NET CARBS
Black coffee	0	0g	0g	0g	0g
7:00 AM 4 ounces leftover steak	270	21g	19g	0g	0g
3 eggs	240	15g	18g	1.5g	1.5g
NOON Butter coffee (Some days you just need that lunchtime butter coffee.)	100	11g	0g	0g	0g
3:00 PM 1 string cheese	80	6g	7g	0g	0g
1 ounce macadamia nuts	200	21g	2g	4g	2g
6:00 PM *Double Bacon Cheeseburger*	820	60g	65g	6g	5g
	1710	134g	111g	11.5g	8.5g
		71.1%	26.2%	2.7%	2%

Double Bacon Cheeseburger

126

DAY 5

	CALORIES	FAT	PROTEIN	CARBS	NET CARBS
Black coffee	0	0g	0g	0g	0g
7:00 AM 4 ounces breakfast sausage	420	38g	20g	2g	2g
1 ounce cheddar cheese	110	9g	7g	0g	0g
1 ounce Brazil nuts	210	21g	4g	3g	1g
NOON 2 servings *Sweet and Spicy Beef Jerky*	300	19.5g	31.5g	1g	1g
1 avocado	235	20g	3g	12g	2g
6:00 PM 4 ounces chicken breast	110	1g	23g	0g	0g
1 tablespoon coconut oil	120	14g	0g	0g	0g
1 cup broccoli	30	0g	1g	4g	2g
1 cup mushrooms	20	0g	3g	3g	1g
	1555	122.5g	92.5g	25g	9g
		70.1%	23.5%	6.4%	2.3%

> Stir-fry! Sauté the chicken in the coconut oil, then add the veggies.

We usually go for fattier cuts of meat, but when we use lean cuts, we add fat to the dish in other ways.

Sweet and Spicy Beef Jerky

186

Megha AND Matt
BAROT GAEDKE

DAY 6

		CALORIES	FAT	PROTEIN	CARBS	NET CARBS
7:00 AM	Black coffee	0	0g	0g	0g	0g
	Microwave Bread	285	25g	10g	6g	2g
	1 tablespoon butter	100	11g	0g	0g	0g
	2 ounces cheddar cheese	220	18g	14g	0g	0g
NOON	1 ounce almond butter	190	16g	6g	7g	3g
	2 stalks celery	15	0g	0g	4g	2g
	2 hard-boiled eggs	160	10g	12g	1g	1g
6:00 PM	*Chipotle Dry-Rub Wings*	507	36g	42.5g	3g	2.5g
	2 cups spinach	10	0g	2g	2g	1g
	Blue cheese dressing	130	13g	1g	1g	1g
		1617	129g	87.5g	24g	12.5g
			72.3%	21.8%	6%	3.1%

Snack lunches are fun sometimes!

74 *Microwave Bread*

142 *Chipotle Dry-Rub Wings*

Omelets are one of our favorite ways to start the day.

DAY 7

		CALORIES	FAT	PROTEIN	CARBS	NET CARBS
7:00 AM	Black coffee	0	0g	0g	0g	0g
	Bacon, spinach, and cheddar omelet	535	40g	36g	2.5g	1.5g
	1 avocado	235	20g	3g	12g	2g
NOON	1 ounce almond butter	190	16g	6g	7g	3g
	2 stalks celery	15	0g	0g	4g	2g
	1 string cheese	80	6g	7g	0g	0g
3:00 PM	1 ounce Brazil nuts	210	21g	4g	3g	1g
6:00 PM	6 ounces rib-eye steak	405	31.5g	28.5g	0g	0g
	2 cups steamed broccoli	60	0g	2g	8g	4g
	1 tablespoon butter	100	11g	0g	0g	0g
		1830	145.5g	86.5g	36.5g	13.5g
			72.7%	19.2%	8.1%	3%

3 eggs, 4 slices bacon, 1 cup spinach, and 1 ounce cheddar cheese

Peanut butter is great, too! We check the ingredient label to make sure no sugar is added.

Medium-rare steaks are our most common dinner. We buy them in bulk to keep costs down.

MEATLESS MARTY

Although challenging, a vegetarian keto diet is possible. Some foods that are great to include as part of a vegetarian keto diet are chia seeds, flax seeds, hemp hearts, nuts, seitan, tofu, and plant-based protein powders. Because vegetarian protein sources are much lower in fat than animal protein sources, it's important to add fat to your meals. When we make vegetarian meals, we always find ourselves adding tablespoons of butter or coconut oil to get the fat content to where we like it.

DAY 1

		CALORIES	FAT	PROTEIN	CARBS	NET CARBS
7:00 AM	Butter coffee	100	11g	0g	0g	0g
	4 scrambled eggs (cooked in the coconut oil)	320	20g	24g	2g	2g
	1 tablespoon coconut oil	120	14g	0g	0g	0g
NOON	*Loaded Cobb Salad* with tofu	650	58g	40g	21g	8g
	6 ounces seitan	240	4g	42g	8g	6g
	1 cup broccoli	30	0g	1g	4g	2g
6:00 PM	1 cup mushrooms	20	0g	3g	3g	1g
	1 tablespoon coconut oil	120	14g	0g	0g	0g
	Peanut Sauce	134	10.5g	6g	6g	4g
		1734	131.5g	116g	44g	23g
			64.9%	25.5%	9.7%	5.1%

> A stir-fry made with coconut oil is a great way to meet your nutrition goals on a vegetarian keto diet.

> Replace the chicken with 6 ounces of tofu.

Loaded Cobb Salad — 162

Peanut Sauce — 244

DAY 2

		CALORIES	FAT	PROTEIN	CARBS	NET CARBS
7:00 AM	Black coffee	0	0g	0g	0g	0g
	2 servings *Toasted Oatmeal*	532	50g	10g	19g	9g
	1 ounce almond butter	190	16g	6g	7g	3g
NOON	2 stalks celery	15	0g	0g	4g	2g
	1 avocado	235	20g	3g	12g	2g
3:00 PM	1 scoop vegan protein powder	120	2g	24g	3g	2g
	1 cup almond milk	35	2.5g	1g	1g	0g
	6 ounces tofu with taco seasoning	160	8g	16g	4g	2g
6:00 PM	2 cups spinach	10	0g	2g	2g	1g
	1 tablespoon olive oil	120	14g	0g	0g	0g
	1 ounce cheddar cheese	110	9g	7g	0g	0g
7:00 PM	2 pieces *Pistachio Coconut Fudge*	245	26g	2.5g	4g	2.5g
		1772	147.5g	71.5g	56g	23.5g
			72.2%	15.6%	12.2%	5.1%

> Getting adequate protein while keeping carbs down can be a challenge for keto vegetarians. We find vegan protein powder helps with that.

> Put everything together for a keto stir-fry.

Toasted Oatmeal — 62

Pistachio Coconut Fudge — 234

		CALORIES	FAT	PROTEIN	CARBS	NET CARBS
7:00 AM	Butter coffee	100	11g	0g	0g	0g
	2 servings *No-Sausage and Gruyère Breakfast Casserole*	309	23g	19g	2g	2g
	1 tablespoon butter	100	11g	0g	0g	0g
	1 scoop vegan protein powder	120	2g	24g	3g	2g
NOON	½ cup coconut milk	180	18g	4g	2g	2g
	1 ounce almonds (to top the smoothie bowl)	180	15g	6g	6g	2g
	2 cups spinach	10	0g	2g	2g	1g
3:00 PM	1 tablespoon olive oil	120	14g	0g	0g	0g
	1 ounce cheddar cheese	110	9g	7g	0g	0g
	6 ounces seitan	240	4g	42g	8g	6g
	1 cup broccoli	30	0g	1g	4g	2g
6:00 PM	1 cup mushrooms	20	0g	3g	3g	1g
	1 tablespoon coconut oil	120	14g	0g	0g	0g
	Peanut Sauce	134	10.5g	6g	6g	4g
		1773	131.5g	114g	36g	22g
			66.4%	25.6%	8.1%	4.9%

> Put everything together for a keto stir-fry.

> Omit the sausage.

Sausage and Gruyère Breakfast Casserole — 58

Peanut Sauce — 244

		CALORIES	FAT	PROTEIN	CARBS	NET CARBS
7:00 AM	Black coffee	0	0g	0g	0g	0g
	Overnight Protein Oats	439	28g	39g	9g	1g
NOON	*Loaded Cobb Salad* with tofu	650	58g	40g	21g	8g
3:00 PM	1 *Breakfast Cookie*	225	17.5g	8.5g	12g	5.5g
	6 ounces tofu with taco seasoning	160	8g	16g	4g	2g
6:00 PM	2 cups spinach	10	0g	2g	2g	1g
	1 tablespoon olive oil	120	14g	0g	0g	0g
	1 ounce cheddar cheese	110	9g	7g	0g	0g
7:00 PM	*Pistachio Coconut Fudge*	123	13g	1.5g	2g	1.5g
		1837	147.5g	114g	50g	19g
			66.9%	23%	10.1%	3.8%

> Put everything together for a keto stir-fry.

Overnight Protein Oats — 50

Loaded Cobb Salad — 162

Breakfast Cookies — 48

Pistachio Coconut Fudge — 234

> These cookies are super filling and great for travel!

DAY 5

		CALORIES	FAT	PROTEIN	CARBS	NET CARBS
7:00 AM	Butter coffee	100	11g	0g	0g	0g
	2 servings *Three-Cheese Spinach Frittata*	296	21g	21g	3g	3g
NOON	1 ounce Brazil nuts	210	21g	4g	3g	1g
	2 stalks celery	15	0g	0g	4g	2g
	1 cup broccoli	30	0g	1g	4g	2g
	2 tablespoons ranch dressing	140	16g	0g	2g	2g
	1 avocado	235	20g	3g	12g	2g
6:00 PM	*Spicy Tofu Fried Rice* (Substitute tofu for the shrimp.)	283	13.5g	32g	13g	9g
	1 *Breakfast Cookie*	225	17.5g	8.5g	12g	5.5g
		1534	120g	69.5g	53g	26.5g
			68.8%	17.7%	13.5%	6.8%

Dip the veggies in the dressing for a flavorful snack lunch.

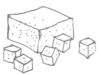

Tofu or other meat alternatives can be used in the majority of the recipes in this book.

Three-Cheese Spinach Frittata — 40

Spicy Shrimp Fried Rice — 134

Breakfast Cookies — 48

DAY 6

		CALORIES	FAT	PROTEIN	CARBS	NET CARBS
7:00 AM	Butter coffee	100	11g	0g	0g	0g
	Microwave Bread	285	25g	10g	6g	2g
	1 tablespoon coconut oil and ¼ teaspoon ground cinnamon	120	14g	0g	0g	0g
NOON	*Loaded Cobb Salad* with tofu	650	58g	40g	21g	8g
6:00 PM	Veggie omelet (3 eggs, 1 cup broccoli, 1 ounce cheddar cheese, and 1 cup spinach)	480	28g	24g	6.5g	3.5g
	Protein Cake with Buttercream Frosting	250	23.5g	10g	3.5g	1g
		1885	159.5g	84g	37g	14.5g
			74.8%	17.5%	7.7%	3%

Microwave Bread with cinnamon!

Microwave Bread — 74

Loaded Cobb Salad — 162

Protein Cake with Buttercream Frosting — 220

DAY 7

		CALORIES	FAT	PROTEIN	CARBS	NET CARBS
7:00 AM	Butter coffee	100	11g	0g	0g	0g
	Overnight Protein Oats	439	28g	39g	9g	1g
	1 avocado	235	20g	3g	12g	2g
	1 ounce almond butter	190	16g	6g	7g	3g
NOON	2 stalks celery	15	0g	0g	4g	2g
	1 string cheese	80	6g	7g	0g	0g
3:00 PM	1 ounce Brazil nuts	210	21g	4g	3g	1g
6:00 PM	*Saag Paneer*	386	31g	15.5g	8.5g	7.5g
		1655	133g	74.5g	43.5g	16.5g
			71.7%	17.9%	10.4%	4%

Overnight Protein Oats — 50

Saag Paneer — 128

Saag paneer is our favorite vegetarian dinner option.

Megha AND Matt BAROT AND GAEDKE

MEAL PLAN 5:
MATT

This meal plan represents a typical week of eating for Matt. He starts every day with two butter coffees. That keeps him productive in the mornings, which is when he gets most of his work done. We hit the gym together at around 10 a.m., fueled by caffeine and butter, and then come home, where Matt has a large meal around lunchtime. He usually has two large meals per day, with the second one being dinner at around 6 p.m. He likes to keep his fat ratio north of 75 percent. That is a personal preference that he has worked out over his three years of eating keto.

			CALORIES	FAT	PROTEIN	CARBS	NET CARBS
DAY 1	6:00 AM	Butter coffee (1 tablespoon butter, 1 tablespoon MCT oil)	220	25g	0g	0g	0g
	9:00 AM	Tea with heavy cream (2 tablespoons heavy cream)	100	10g	0g	0g	0g
		2 servings *Sausage and Gruyère Breakfast Casserole*	564	44g	37g	2g	2g
	NOON	1 ounce macadamia nuts	200	21g	2g	4g	2g
		3 ounces smoked salmon	150	8g	18g	0.5g	0.5g
		10 ounces rib-eye steak	675	52.5g	47.5g	0g	0g
	6:00 PM	2 cups steamed broccoli	60	0g	2g	8g	4g
		1 tablespoon butter	100	11g	0g	0g	0g
		2 servings *Pistachio Coconut Fudge*	245	26g	2.5g	4g	2.5g
	8:00 PM	Tea	0	0g	0g	0g	0g
			2314	197.5g	109g	18.5g	11g
				77.7%	19.1%	3.2%	1.9%

> Smoked salmon is a great way to add protein and omega-3 fats to your diet.

58

Sausage and Gruyère Breakfast Casserole

234

Pistachio Coconut Fudge

> Matt likes having one or two fat bombs per day to keep his fat ratio high.

DAY 2

			CALORIES	FAT	PROTEIN	CARBS	NET CARBS
6:00 AM	Butter coffee (1 tablespoon butter, 1 tablespoon MCT oil)		220	25g	0g	0g	0g
9:00 AM	Butter coffee (1 tablespoon butter, 1 tablespoon MCT oil)		220	25g	0g	0g	0g
NOON	1 tin sardines packed in olive oil		150	11g	13g	0g	0g
	2 slices *The Best Keto Bread*		225	20g	9g	5g	3g
	2 tablespoons butter		200	22g	0g	0g	0g
	2 ounces prosciutto		120	6g	16g	2g	2g
	2 hard-boiled eggs		160	10g	12g	1g	1g
6:00 PM	*Loaded Cobb Salad*		778	64g	43g	15g	5g
7:00 PM	1 ounce macadamia nuts		200	21g	2g	4g	2g
			2273	204g 79%	95g 16.4%	27g 4.7%	13g 2.2%

> This is a typical lunch that Matt would pack for work at his old office job.

Matt starts most mornings with a fat fast. That is when you consume nothing but fat until the early afternoon, when you have a meal.

The Best Keto Bread — 76

Loaded Cobb Salad — 162

DAY 3

			CALORIES	FAT	PROTEIN	CARBS	NET CARBS
6:00 AM	Butter coffee (1 tablespoon butter, 1 tablespoon MCT oil)		220	25g	0g	0g	0g
9:00 AM	Tea with heavy cream (2 tablespoons heavy cream)		100	10g	0g	0g	0g
NOON	3 servings *Sausage and Gruyère Breakfast Casserole*		846	66g	56g	3.5g	3.5g
	1 ounce almonds		180	15g	6g	6g	2g
6:00 PM	2 servings *Crispy Chicken Thighs with Pan Sauce*		616	42g	71g	6.5g	6g
	2 ounces kimchi		15	0g	1g	2g	1g
7:00 PM	Fatty hot chocolate		265	29g	2g	4g	1g
			2242	187g 72.7%	136g 23.5%	22g 3.8%	13.5g 2.3%

> 1 cup almond milk, 1 tablespoon cocoa powder, 1 tablespoon butter, and 1 tablespoon MCT oil

leftover

Sausage and Gruyère Breakfast Casserole

108

Crispy Chicken Thighs with Pan Sauce

Kimchi is a great way to get some fermented foods into your diet.

DAY 4

			CALORIES	FAT	PROTEIN	CARBS	NET CARBS
6:00 AM	Butter coffee (1 tablespoon butter, 1 tablespoon MCT oil)		220	25g	0g	0g	0g
9:00 AM	Butter coffee (1 tablespoon butter, 1 tablespoon MCT oil)		220	25g	0g	0g	0g
NOON	*Easy Eggs Benedict*		651	55g	26.5g	14.5g	5g
	2 servings *Pistachio Coconut Fudge*		245	26g	2.5g	4g	2.5g
6:00 PM	10-ounce rib-eye steak		675	52.5g	47.5g	0g	0g
	1 ounce Parmesan cheese		100	7g	9g	1g	1g
	Asparagus with Goat Cheese and Sunflower Seeds		148	10g	7.5g	6.5g	4g
			2259	200.5g 79.1%	93g 16.3%	26g 4.6%	12.5g 2.2%

When we buy rib-eye, we look for the most marbled cuts, which indicate a higher fat percentage... and better taste.

Easy Eggs Benedict — 54

leftover

Pistachio Coconut Fudge

Asparagus with Goat Cheese and Sunflower Seeds — 200

Megha BAROT *AND* Matt GAEDKE

DAY 5

			CALORIES	FAT	PROTEIN	CARBS	NET CARBS
6:00 AM	Butter coffee	(1 tablespoon butter, 1 tablespoon MCT oil)	220	25g	0g	0g	0g
9:00 AM	Butter coffee	(1 tablespoon butter, 1 tablespoon MCT oil)	220	25g	0g	0g	0g
	Bacon, spinach, and cheddar cheese omelet		535	40g	36g	2.5g	1.5g
NOON	2 slices *The Best Keto Bread*		225	20g	9g	5g	3g
	2 tablespoons butter		200	22g	0g	0g	0g
6:00 PM	*Chipotle Dry-Rub Wings*		507	36g	42.5g	3g	2.5g
	2 servings *Pistachio Coconut Fudge*		245	26g	2.5g	4g	2.5g
			2152	194g	90g	14.5g	9.5g
				80.7%	16.6%	2.7%	1.8%

> 3 eggs, 2 slices bacon, 1 cup spinach, and 1 ounce cheddar cheese

> Wing night! We make wings and watch a movie for date night every couple of weeks.

The Best Keto Bread — 76

Chipotle Dry-Rub Wings — 142

Pistachio Coconut Fudge — leftover

DAY 6

			CALORIES	FAT	PROTEIN	CARBS	NET CARBS
6:00 AM	Butter coffee	(1 tablespoon butter, 1 tablespoon MCT oil)	220	25g	0g	0g	0g
9:00 AM	Butter coffee	(1 tablespoon butter, 1 tablespoon MCT oil)	220	25g	0g	0g	0g
	4 prosciutto and mozzarella roll-ups		240	15g	28g	1g	1g
NOON	4 hard-boiled eggs		320	20g	24g	2g	2g
	1 ounce Brazil nuts		210	21g	4g	3g	1g
6:00 PM	8-ounce ground bison *Double Bacon Cheeseburger*		820	60g	65g	6g	5g
	Tea with heavy cream (2 tablespoons heavy cream)		100	10g	0g	0g	0g
			2130	176g	121g	12g	9g
				74.9%	22.9%	2.3%	1.7%

> Use ½ ounce each of prosciutto and mozzarella per roll-up.

> Substitute ground bison for the beef. Bison is delicious and can be cooked rare, just the way we like it.

Double Bacon Cheeseburger — 126

DAY 7

			CALORIES	FAT	PROTEIN	CARBS	NET CARBS
6:00 AM	Butter coffee	(1 tablespoon butter, 1 tablespoon MCT oil)	220	25g	0g	0g	0g
9:00 AM	Butter coffee	(1 tablespoon butter, 1 tablespoon MCT oil)	220	25g	0g	0g	0g
	3 servings *Sausage and Gruyère Breakfast Casserole*		846	66g	56g	3.5g	3.5g
NOON	1 ounce almond butter		190	16g	6g	7g	3g
	2 stalks celery		15	0g	0g	4g	2g
6:00 PM	*Loaded Cobb Salad*		778	64g	43g	15g	5g
7:00 PM	*Protein Cake with Buttercream Frosting*		250	23.5g	10g	3.5g	1g
			2519	219.5g	115g	33g	14.5g
				76.9%	17.9%	5.1%	2.3%

> Breakfast casseroles and frittatas are always part of our meal preps.

Sausage and Gruyère Breakfast Casserole — 58

Loaded Cobb Salad — 162

Protein Cake with Buttercream Frosting — 220

MEGHA

Megha has never been a huge coffee drinker, but she likes to start the morning with a warm, high-fat drink, so she usually makes a butter chai tea. She is a veggie lover, so she tries to fit in as many vegetables as possible. Most days she eats just two large meals, but she is also a huge snacker. That usually means a fat bomb or a little snack plate between meals or a spoonful of peanut butter before bed. Her carb intake is higher than Matt's most of the time, and her fat intake is lower. Remember, finding what works best for your body is the key!

(3 hard-boiled eggs, 2 tablespoons mayo, ½ tablespoon curry powder)

> Megha likes to limit her caffeine intake, so most mornings she drinks this butter chai tea.

> Curry egg salad is Megha's go-to snack.

> 3 hard-boiled eggs, 2 tablespoons mayo, ½ tablespoon curry powder

> Megha likes making an array of roasted veggies as a side dish for dinner. Just roast at 400°F for 15 minutes.

> We split desserts and binge-watch TV shows. It's a problem.

DAY 1

			CALORIES	FAT	PROTEIN	CARBS	NET CARBS
7:00 AM	Butter chai tea (1 tablespoon butter)		100	11g	0g	0g	0g
10:00 AM	Curry egg salad		430	35g	18g	1.5g	1.5g
2:00 PM	*Sausage and Gruyère Breakfast Casserole*		282	22g	18.5g	1g	1g
	½ avocado		117	10g	1.5g	6g	1g
	Crispy Chicken Thighs with Pan Sauce		308	21g	35.5g	3g	2.5g
	½ cup radishes		10	0g	0.5g	2g	1g
6:00 PM	1 cup broccoli		30	0g	1g	4g	2g
	1 cup cauliflower		30	0.5g	2g	5g	3g
	1 tablespoon olive oil		120	14g	0g	0g	0g
8:00 PM	½ serving *Snickerdoodle Cream Cheesecake*		201	18g	5.5g	6g	2.5g
			1628	131.5g	82.5g	28.5g	14.5g
				72.7%	20.3%	7%	3.6%

Sausage and Gruyère Breakfast Casserole — 58

Crispy Chicken Thighs with Pan Sauce — 108

Snickerdoodle Cream Cheesecake — 214

DAY 2

			CALORIES	FAT	PROTEIN	CARBS	NET CARBS
7:00 AM	Butter chai tea (1 tablespoon butter)		100	11g	0g	0g	0g
10:00 AM	Butter chai tea (1 tablespoon butter)		100	11g	0g	0g	0g
2:00 PM	½ serving *Loaded Cobb Salad*		389	32g	21.5g	7.5g	2.5g
6:00 PM	6 ounces crispy duck breast (sear fat side down)		363	20g	43g	0g	0g
	2 ounces kimchi		15	0g	1g	2g	1g
	2 ounces raw goat milk cheese		200	18g	14g	1g	1g
	½ avocado		117	10g	1.5g	6g	1g
9:00 PM	2 tablespoons peanut butter		190	16g	8g	7g	4g
			1474	118g	89g	23.5g	9.5g
				70.2%	23.5%	6.2%	2.5%

We like to get duck breast whenever we can find it. The skin makes it super fatty and delicious.

162

Loaded Cobb Salad

DAY 3

			CALORIES	FAT	PROTEIN	CARBS	NET CARBS
7:00 AM	Butter chai tea (1 tablespoon butter)		100	11g	0g	0g	0g
10:00 AM	2 servings *Savory Zucchini Cheddar Waffles*		584	38g	40g	28g	18g
	2 tablespoons sour cream		50	5g	1g	1g	1g
2:00 PM	*Curry Chicken Salad*		339	14g	25.5g	2.5g	1.5g
	½ avocado		117	10g	1.5g	6g	1g
6:00 PM	*Chipotle Dry-Rub Wings*		507	36g	42.5g	3g	2.5g
	2 stalks celery		15	0g	0g	4g	2g
	Blue cheese dressing		130	13g	1g	1g	0g
			1842	127g	111.5g	45.5g	26g
				64.5%	25.2%	10.3%	5.9%

Wing night is what we live for.

42

160

142

Savory Zucchini Cheddar Waffles

Curry Chicken Salad

Chipotle Dry-Rub Wings

DAY 4

			CALORIES	FAT	PROTEIN	CARBS	NET CARBS
7:00 AM	Butter chai tea (1 tablespoon butter)		100	11g	0g	0g	0g
10:00 AM	*Green Power Smoothie*		416	27g	35g	7g	4g
2:00 PM	2 ounces raw goat milk cheese		200	18g	14g	1g	1g
	2 ounces pepperoni		260	24g	12g	0g	0g
6:00 PM	6 ounces rib-eye steak		405	31.5g	28.5g	0g	0g
	Asparagus with Goat Cheese and Sunflower Seeds		148	10g	7.5g	6.5g	4g
8:00 PM	2 *Peanut Butter Hemp Heart Cookies*		240	19.5g	10.5g	8g	3.5g
			1769	141g	107.5g	22.5g	12.5g
				70.9%	24%	5%	2.8%

Megha often starts or ends her day with a smoothie or a smoothie bowl of some kind.

172

200

230

Green Power Smoothie

Asparagus with Goat Cheese and Sunflower Seeds

Peanut Butter Hemp Heart Cookies

DAY 5

			CALORIES	FAT	PROTEIN	CARBS	NET CARBS
7:00 AM	Butter chai tea	(1 tablespoon butter)	100	11g	0g	0g	0g
10:00 AM	*Mocha Protein Keto Coffee*		361	24g	37g	4g	2g
	4 ounces leftover steak		270	21g	19g	0g	0g
2:00 PM	2 cups steamed broccoli		60	0g	2g	8g	4g
	1 tablespoon butter		100	11g	0g	0g	0g
	1 ounce prosciutto		60	3g	8g	1g	1g
	1 ounce salami		110	10g	6g	0g	0g
	1 ounce chorizo		100	8g	7g	1g	1g
6:00 PM	1 ounce goat cheese		100	9g	7g	0.5g	0.5g
	1 ounce Brie		110	10g	5g	0g	0g
	1 ounce Gouda		110	9g	7g	0g	0g
	Giant Skillet Cookie for Two		406	38.5g	9.5g	11g	7.5g
			1887	154.5g	107.5g	25.5g	16g
				72.3%	22.4%	5.3%	3.3%

> Try this! Put together a fancy charcuterie board and watch a classic movie.

> Perfect for date night! Yeah...we don't leave the house much.

Mocha Protein Keto Coffee | 66

Giant Skillet Cookie for Two | 216

DAY 6

			CALORIES	FAT	PROTEIN	CARBS	NET CARBS
7:00 AM	Butter chai tea	(1 tablespoon butter)	100	11g	0g	0g	0g
10:00 AM	2 *Raspberry Fiber Muffins*		262	21g	8.5g	22g	1.5g
	2 tablespoons coconut oil		240	28g	0g	0g	0g
2:00 PM	*Creamy White Chili*		278	18g	24g	3.5g	3g
6:00 PM	*Saag Paneer*		386	31g	15.5g	8.5g	7.5g
9:00 PM	2 tablespoons peanut butter		190	16g	8g	7g	4g
			1456	125g	56g	41g	16g
				74.4%	14.8%	10.8%	4.2%

> Megha is one of those people who eats peanut butter right out of the jar.

Raspberry Fiber Muffins | 78

Creamy White Chili | 104

Saag Paneer | 128

DAY 7

			CALORIES	FAT	PROTEIN	CARBS	NET CARBS
7:00 AM	Butter chai tea	(1 tablespoon butter)	100	11g	0g	0g	0g
	Microwave Bread		285	25g	10g	6g	2g
10:00 AM	2 eggs		160	10g	12g	1g	1g
	2 slices bacon		90	7g	5g	0g	0g
2:00 PM	*Caprese Chicken Skillet*		226	12g	26.5g	3.5g	2.5g
	6 ounces rib-eye steak		405	31.5g	28.5g	0g	0g
	1 cup broccoli		30	0g	1g	4g	2g
6:00 PM	1 cup cauliflower		30	0.5g	2g	5g	3g
	2 ounces kimchi		15	0g	1g	2g	1g
	1 tablespoon olive oil		120	14g	0g	0g	0g
7:00 PM	½ *Blackberry Mini Cheesecake*		241	24g	4g	3.5g	2.5g
			1702	135g	90g	25g	14g
				72.5%	21.5%	6%	3.3%

> Roast the broccoli and cauliflower together at 400°F for 15 minutes.

> This is a cookbook, so we put ½ serving...but really, who eats only half a mini cheesecake? Megha ate the whole thing.

Microwave Bread | 74

Caprese Chicken Skillet | 156

Blackberry Mini Cheesecakes | 224

SUGGESTED READING

While putting the ketogenic diet into practice is simple, getting a better understanding of the underlying science can be hugely beneficial. Here we've provided a list of books and websites that you can use to further your knowledge. This cookbook gives you more than a hundred recipes that are perfect for your keto journey, but for detailed information on what a ketogenic diet is and why ketosis is a great state for your body to be in, we recommend that you delve into some of these more comprehensive resources.

Books

- *The Case Against Sugar* by Gary Taubes

- *Good Calories, Bad Calories: Fats, Carbs, and the Controversial Science of Diet and Health* by Gary Taubes

- *The Obesity Code: Unlocking the Secrets of Weight Loss* by Dr. Jason Fung

- *Why We Get Fat: And What to Do About It* by Gary Taubes

Websites

- KetoConnect.net *(our food blog; hit the "Start Here" drop-down menu for a discussion of some of the basics of the keto diet)*

- Reddit.com/r/keto

RESOURCE GUIDE

The following is a list of ingredients and prepared foods we commonly use and the brands we prefer to purchase. They can be found in most grocery stores. For more information about some of these ingredients, or for information about ingredients not listed below, check the ingredients section on pages 12 to 21.

Staple Ingredients

Apple cider vinegar, raw and unfiltered
Bragg

Baking chocolate, unsweetened
Baker's

BBQ Sauce
G Hughes Smokehouse sugar-free BBQ sauce

Chicken broth, low-sodium
Imagine organic free-range broth

Chocolate chips, sugar-free
Lily's

Coconut aminos (a soy sauce alternative)
Bragg

Coconut cream and coconut milk
Thai Kitchen

Ketchup, reduced-sugar
Heinz

Maple syrup, sugar-free

> *Know Foods Know Better Syrup* (the best choice, but not available in most grocery stores)

> *Log Cabin Sugar-Free* (readily available at grocery stores, but not our first choice because it contains unsavory sweeteners and artificial colors)

Marinara sauce, low-carb
> *Rao's*

Mayonnaise, made with avocado oil
> *Primal Kitchen*

MCT oil and MCT powder

> *Perfect Keto MCT Oil Powder* (available at perfectketo.com and on Amazon.com)

> *Zenwise* (available at zenwisehealth.com and on Amazon.com)

Meats
> *Applegate natural uncured beef hot dogs*

> *BUBBA burgers* (Angus beef and turkey)

Peanut butter
> *Crazy Richard's*

Pork rinds
> *Mac's*
> *Utz*

Tortillas
> *Mission Carb Balance*

Snack Suggestions

Here are some of our favorite ready-made snack options.

Bars
  Keto Bars (the best choice, but not available in grocery stores)
  Quest Bars (readily available in grocery stores)

Crackers
  Flackers (organic flaxseed crackers)

Ice cream
  So Delicious Dairy Free, No Sugar Added

Jerky
  Keto Carne (the best choice, but not available in grocery stores)

Pili nuts

Pizza
  Realgood

Sardines, wild-caught
  Wild Planet

Yogurt, almond milk
  Kite Hill

RECIPE INDEX

Wake-up Call

Protein Waffles

Three-Cheese
Spinach Frittata

Savory Zucchini
Cheddar Waffles

Five-Star
Breakfast Sandwich

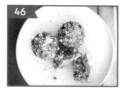
Chorizo Cotija
Morning Muffins

Breakfast Cookies

Overnight Protein Oats

Breakfast Roll-ups

Easy Eggs Benedict

Golden Gate Granola

Sausage and Gruyère
Breakfast Casserole

Diner Pancakes

Toasted Oatmeal

Iced Bulletproof
Coffee Frappé

Mocha Protein Keto
Coffee

Chapter 2

Fresh Baked

English Muffins
70

Cheddar and Thyme Cornbread
72

Microwave Bread
74

The Best Keto Bread
76

Raspberry Fiber Muffins
78

Cheddar Jalapeño Bagels
80

Low-Carb Dinner Rolls
82

Cinnamon Walnut Scones
84

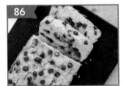
Chocolate Chip Zucchini Bread
86

Cheesy Chicken Breadsticks
88

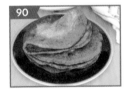
Navajo Fry Bread
90

Coconut Flour Tortillas
92

Classic Comfort Foods

Chicken Popper Casserole
96

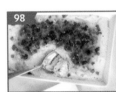
Loaded Cauliflower
98

Spicy Cauliflower Bites
100

Spaghetti with Meat Sauce
102

Creamy White Chili
104

Chicken Tenders
106

Crispy Chicken Thighs with Pan Sauce
108

Mexican Chorizo Casserole
110

Bacon and Crab Mac
and Cheese

Chicken Noodle-less
Soup

Creamy Chicken
Alfredo

Southern Baked
Chicken

Mama's Meatloaf

Takeout Favorites

Spicy Tuna Hand Rolls

Double Bacon
Cheeseburger

Saag Paneer

Thai Yellow Chicken
Curry

Buffalo Chicken Crust
Pizza

Spicy Shrimp Fried
Rice

Chocolate Almond
Butter Shake

Thin-Crust Skillet
Pizza

Steak Quesadillas

Chipotle Dry-Rub
Wings

Beef Satay Skewers

Cheese Shell
Mini Tacos

Philly Food Cart Gyros

Sticky Sesame
Chicken

Fresh Fixin's

Turkey Bacon Club
154

Caprese Chicken Skillet
156

Baja Fish Soft Tacos
158

Curry Chicken Salad
160

Loaded Cobb Salad
162

Coconut Shrimp
164

Fried Red Snapper
166

California Collard Wrap
168

Strawberry Coconut Smoothie
170

Green Power Smoothie
172

Raspberry Lime Ice Pops
174

Sides & Munchies

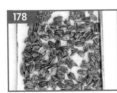
Candied Georgia Pecans
178

Fathead Crackers
180

Mexican Layer Dip
182

Buffalo Chicken Dip
184

Sweet and Spicy Beef Jerky
186

Charlie's Energy Balls
188

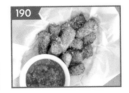
Bar Side Mozzarella Sticks
190

Salami Chips with Pesto
192

Radical Radish Chips

Cheesy Broccoli and Bacon

Hush Puppies

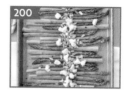
Asparagus with Goat Cheese and Sunflower Seeds

Chipotle Cauliflower Mash

Cilantro Lime Rice

Decadent Desserts

Chocolate Protein Truffles

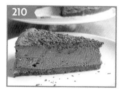
Death by Chocolate Cheesecake

No-Churn Peanut Butter Ice Cream

Snickerdoodle Cream Cheesecake

Giant Skillet Cookie for Two

Flourless Chocolate Cake

Protein Cake with Buttercream Frosting

Chewy Chocolate Chip Cookies

Blackberry Mini Cheesecakes

Extreme Fudge Brownies

Coconut Chocolate Cookies

Peanut Butter Hemp Heart Cookies

County Fair Cinnamon
Donuts

Pistachio Coconut
Fudge

Strawberry
Shortcakes

Vanilla Egg Custard

Instant Protein
Ice Cream

Condiments

Peanut Sauce

BBQ Sauce

Homemade Chipotle
Mayo

Maple Cinnamon
Almond Butter

Strawberry Chia Seed
Jam

ALLERGEN INDEX

O - OPTION

RECIPES	PAGE	🥛	⊘	🥜	🥦	👍	✕
Protein Waffles	38				✓	✓	
Three-Cheese Spinach Frittata	40			✓	✓		
Savory Zucchini Cheddar Waffles	42			✓	✓		
Five-Star Breakfast Sandwich	44					✓	
Chorizo Cotija Morning Muffins	46			✓			
Breakfast Cookies	48	✓	✓		✓		
Overnight Protein Oats	50		✓	✓		✓	✓
Breakfast Roll-ups	52			✓			
Easy Eggs Benedict	54			✓			
Golden Gate Granola	56		✓	✓	✓		✓
Sausage and Gruyère Breakfast Casserole	58			✓			✓
Diner Pancakes	60			O	✓		
Toasted Oatmeal	62	O	✓		✓		✓
Iced Bulletproof Coffee Frappé	64		✓	✓		✓	
Mocha Protein Keto Coffee	66		✓	✓		✓	
English Muffins	70		✓	✓	✓		
Cheddar and Thyme Cornbread	72				✓		
Microwave Bread	74				✓	✓	
The Best Keto Bread	76				✓		
Raspberry Fiber Muffins	78			✓	✓		
Cheddar Jalapeño Bagels	80			✓	✓		
Low-Carb Dinner Rolls	82			✓	✓		
Cinnamon Walnut Scones	84	✓			✓		
Chocolate Chip Zucchini Bread	86	✓			✓		
Cheesy Chicken Breadsticks	88			✓			
Navajo Fry Bread	90	✓		✓	✓		
Coconut Flour Tortillas	92	✓		✓	✓		
Chicken Popper Casserole	96		✓	✓		✓	
Loaded Cauliflower	98		✓	✓			
Spicy Cauliflower Bites	100	✓	✓	✓	✓	✓	
Spaghetti with Meat Sauce	102	✓	✓	✓			
Creamy White Chili	104		✓	✓			✓
Chicken Tenders	106						
Crispy Chicken Thighs with Pan Sauce	108		✓	✓			✓
Mexican Chorizo Casserole	110		✓	✓		✓	✓
Bacon and Crab Mac and Cheese	112		✓	✓			
Chicken Noodle-less Soup	114		✓	✓			
Creamy Chicken Alfredo	116		✓	✓			
Southern Baked Chicken	118	✓	✓	✓			
Mama's Meatloaf	120	✓	✓	✓			✓
Spicy Tuna Hand Rolls	124	✓		✓			
Double Bacon Cheeseburger	126		✓	✓			
Saag Paneer	128		✓	✓	✓		✓
Thai Yellow Chicken Curry	130	✓	✓	✓			✓
Buffalo Chicken Crust Pizza	132			✓			
Spicy Shrimp Fried Rice	134	✓		✓			✓
Chocolate Almond Butter Shake	136		✓		✓	✓	
Thin-Crust Skillet Pizza	138		✓	✓		✓	

RECIPES	PAGE	🥛	⊘	🥜	🥦	👍	🍴
Steak Quesadillas	140			✓			
Chipotle Dry-Rub Wings	142	✓	✓	✓			✓
Beef Satay Skewers	144	✓	✓	✓			
Cheese Shell Mini Tacos	146			✓			
Philly Food Cart Gyros	148	✓	✓	✓			
Sticky Sesame Chicken	150	✓	✓	✓			
Turkey Bacon Club	154						
Caprese Chicken Skillet	156		✓	✓			
Baja Fish Soft Tacos	158			✓			
Curry Chicken Salad	160			✓			✓
Loaded Cobb Salad	162			✓			
Coconut Shrimp	164	✓		✓			
Fried Red Snapper	166	✓	✓	✓			
California Collard Wrap	168	✓		✓			
Strawberry Coconut Smoothie	170		✓	✓		✓	
Green Power Smoothie	172		✓	✓		✓	
Raspberry Lime Ice Pops	174	✓	✓	✓	✓	✓	
Candied Georgia Pecans	178	✓			✓		✓
Fathead Crackers	180				✓		
Mexican Layer Dip	182		✓	✓			
Buffalo Chicken Dip	184		✓	✓		✓	
Sweet and Spicy Beef Jerky	186	✓	✓	✓			✓
Charlie's Energy Balls	188						
Bar Side Mozzarella Sticks	190			✓			
Salami Chips with Pesto	192		✓				
Radical Radish Chips	194	✓	✓	✓	✓		
Cheesy Broccoli and Bacon	196		✓	✓		✓	✓
Hush Puppies	198	✓		✓			
Asparagus with Goat Cheese and Sunflower Seeds	200		✓	✓	✓	✓	
Chipotle Cauliflower Mash	202		✓	✓	✓		✓
Cilantro Lime Rice	204		✓	✓	✓	✓	
Chocolate Protein Truffles	208		✓		✓		
Death by Chocolate Cheesecake	210			✓	✓		
No-Churn Peanut Butter Ice Cream	212			✓	✓		
Snickerdoodle Cream Cheesecake	214			✓	✓		
Giant Skillet Cookie for Two	216						
Flourless Chocolate Cake	218			✓	✓		
Protein Cake with Buttercream Frosting	220			✓	✓		✓
Chewy Chocolate Chip Cookies	222						
Blackberry Mini Cheesecakes	224				✓		
Extreme Fudge Brownies	226			✓	✓		
Coconut Chocolate Cookies	228			✓	✓		
Peanut Butter Hemp Heart Cookies	230	✓		✓	✓	✓	
County Fair Cinnamon Donuts	232			✓	✓		
Pistachio Coconut Fudge	234		✓		✓		
Strawberry Shortcakes	236				✓		
Vanilla Egg Custard	238			✓	✓	✓	
Instant Protein Ice Cream	240		✓			✓	
Peanut Sauce	244	✓	✓	✓	✓		
BBQ Sauce	246	✓	✓	✓			
Homemade Chipotle Mayo	248	✓		✓	✓		
Maple Cinnamon Almond Butter	250	✓	✓		✓		✓
Strawberry Chia Seed Jam	252	✓	✓	✓	✓		

GENERAL INDEX